STUDY GUIDE TO ACCOMPANY

THIRD CANADIAN EDITION

abnormal
PSYCHOLOGY

GERALD C. DAVISON
University of Southern California

KIRK R. BLANKSTEIN
University of Toronto

GORDON L. FLETT
York University

JOHN M. NEALE
State University of New York at Stony Brook

Prepared by

JOHN S. CONKLIN
Camosun College

WILEY

John Wiley & Sons Canada, Ltd.

Library and Archives Canada Cataloguing in Publication

Conklin, John
   Study guide to accompany Abnormal psychology, third Canadian edition / John Conklin. —3rd Canadian ed.

Supplement to: Abnormal psychology.
ISBN 978-0-470-15523-3

   1. Psychology, Pathological—Problems, exercises, etc. I. Title.

RC454.A255 2007 Suppl. 1   616.89   C2007-906445-0

Production Credits
Acquisitions Editor: Rodney Burke
Publisher: Veronica Visentin
Vice President, Publishing Services: Karen Bryan
Editorial Manager: Karen Staudinger
Marketing Manager: Joan Lewis-Milne
Developmental Editor: Zoë Craig
Cover Design: Natalia Burobina
Typesetting: Thomson Digital [A Division of Thomson Press (India) Ltd.]
Printing & Binding: Quebecor World Inc.

Printed and bound in United States of America.
1 2 3 4 5   QW   11 10 09 08 07

John Wiley & Sons Canada, Ltd.
6045 Freemont Blvd.
Mississauga, Ontario L5R 4J3

Visit our website at www.wiley.ca

To The Students

This Study Guide is designed to help you study *Abnormal Psychology*, Third Canadian Edition by Davison, Blankstein, Flett & Neale. Each chapter in this guide provides a variety of aids to make your study easier and more effective.

Overview sections place the chapter in context by describing its relationship to the chapters that precede and follow it.

Chapter Summary sections, not surprisingly, summarize the chapter.

Essential Concepts list the important ideas or concepts to be learned in the chapter.

Key Terms provide a place for you to write in definitions of technical words introduced in the chapter. Typically, these terms are boldfaced in the text.

Study Questions are questions for you to answer as you read each section of the text. The Study Guide provides space for you to write your answers to each question. Research indicates that actually writing the answers is an effective way to study.

Self-Test provides a way for you to check your knowledge of the chapter. The Self-Test questions cover the content specified by the Study Questions, except for an occasional asterisked (*) test question.

The Study Guide begins with a chapter on *Studying Abnormal Psychology (and in Other Courses Too)*. This chapter is based on my experiences helping students improve their study skills. It describes a study method (SQ4R) you can use to improve your study skills. It also provides suggestions for coping with common study problems.

Abnormal psychology is a fascinating, but complex, topic for many students. Hopefully, this Study Guide will make your study easier and more effective.

Contents

Studying in This Course (and in Other Courses Too)

I'm convinced—though it might be hard to prove—that few students get bad grades because they're dumb. There is little in the average college curriculum (including abnormal psychology) that's beyond the intellectual capacities of most college students. I'm convinced most students get poor grades because they don't know how to study.

Being a student is a job. The hours are long and the pay is nonexistent, but it's still a job. The payoff is the knowledge you gain and the grades you get. You've been at this "job" for many years, and you're probably not through with it. If this is your job, you might consider how to become really good at it. Are you learning? Are you working efficiently and getting the results you should?

This Study Guide incorporates features to help you develop good study skills. If you spend a little time consciously working on your study skills, you can help the process along.

This chapter is intended to help you review and improve your study skills. The first part of the chapter describes a system, SQ4R, which you can use in this or almost any course. The second part of the chapter contains suggestions for dealing with common study problems.

THE SQ4R STUDY SYSTEM

As you begin to study a new chapter, follow this plan.

SURVEY

First, survey the entire chapter briefly. Spend a few minutes getting a general idea of the material. Look over the titles, pictures, introduction, and summary in the text. Read the overview, chapter summary, and essential concepts in this Study Guide. While doing so, ask yourself what you will be studying. Figure out how the text is organized to cover the topic. Don't read the chapter in detail yet. This brief survey will help you focus your attention and become familiar with new vocabulary and concepts. Research suggests that initially surveying the chapter can reduce your overall study time by 40 percent.

QUESTION

Look at the first portion of the chapter and ask yourself what you are about to study. The study questions in this Study Guide will help you formulate this question. In other courses, take the main heading or topic and turn it into a question.

READ

Read the first portion of the text, looking for the answer to your question. It is important that you actively seek the answer as you read. Deliberately try *not* to read every word. Instead, read for answers.

Typically a text will make several points about each general topic. Look for words indicating these points, such as, "first," "furthermore," or "finally." Generally, a paragraph contains one idea. Additional paragraphs may elaborate on or illustrate the point. You may find it helpful to number each point in the text as you find it.

WRITE

Write down the answer in the space below the study question in your guide. In other courses, take study notes. This step is critical. By writing the answer, you confirm that you actually understand it. Occasionally, when you try to write down your answer, you'll discover you don't understand the idea well enough to put it into words. That's okay. Go back and read some more until you figure it out.

As you write the answer, strive to use as few words as possible. Being concise is important. Try to come up with a few key words that convey the idea. When you can condense a long portion of text into a few key words that express the whole idea, you know you understand the idea clearly. The few key words you write down will be meaningful to you so you will remember them. Do not write complete sentences or elaborate excessively. The fewer words you can use, the better you probably understand and will remember the concept.

When you finish, go on to the next study question. Read, write, and repeat until you finish.

RECITE

After you finish the chapter, go back and quiz yourself. Do this aloud. Actively speaking and listening to yourself will help you remember. Look at each question and try to repeat the answer without looking. Cover your answers with a sheet of paper so you don't peek accidentally. If you've done the earlier steps well, this won't take much time.

REVIEW

Set aside a few minutes every week to recite the material again. Put several questions together and try to recite all the answers to a whole general topic. If you do this regularly, you'll find it takes little time to refresh yourself for an exam.

Get with a classmate to quiz each other, or ask a friend to read the questions and tell you if your answers make sense. This step helps you understand (not just memorize) the material. As you discuss answers with someone else, you develop new ways of looking at the material. This can be especially helpful when the test questions aren't phrased quite the way you expected.

The technique above is one variation of a study method called "SQ4R" (Survey, Question, Read, Write, Recite, Review). If you're not used to it, it may seem a bit complicated at first. If you check around, though, you will find that the "good" students are already using it or a similar system. Research suggests that SQ4R works. It takes a bit of extra effort to get used to, but remember that studying is a skill and that learning any skill (like typing, driving, and playing ball) takes time and practice. You will find, though, that your efforts will pay off in this and in your other courses.

COPING WITH STUDY PROBLEMS

The previous section of this chapter described an active study technique that has proven useful to many students. This section talks about common study complaints and what to do about them.

FINDING THE TIME

Does it seem like you never have time to study—or that you study all the time and still aren't getting results? Admittedly, study takes time, but let's look at the matter.

The traditional rule of thumb is that you should study two hours outside class for every hour in class. If that sounds like a lot, consider this. The average college student class load is 15 semester hours. If you study two hours for each class hour, that's 30 additional hours for a "work week" of 45 hours.

If you have trouble finding that 45 hours, it's time to look at how you spend your time. Make a "time log." You can copy the time log at the end of this chapter or make one of your own. Use it to record how you spend your time for a week or so. Don't try to change what you're doing. Just record it.

After a week or so, stop and look at how you're using your time. There are 90 hours between 8 a.m. and 11 p.m. in a six-day week. If you devote half those hours to the "job" of being a student, you'll have 45 for study and 45 hours left over. That's your free time.

You may want to schedule your time differently. You'll need to decide what works for your style and situation. If you set up a schedule, be sure to include time for things you really enjoy, as well as time to eat, do your laundry, etc.

Schedule adequate study time and actually spend it studying. If you get everything done and have time left over, use it to get ahead in one of your classes. When your study time is over, you should be able to enjoy other activities without worrying about your "job."

GETTING STARTED

Do you find it difficult to actually get down to work when it's study time? Many students find it helpful to find or make a specific study place. It could be a desk in your room, the library, or any place where you won't be disturbed and have access to your books and materials.

Use your study place *only* to study. If it *has* to be a place where you do other things, change it in some way when you use it to study. For example, if you use the kitchen table, clear it off and place a study light on it before you start to study. If you're interrupted, leave your study place until the interruption is over and you can return to studying.

If you do this, you'll soon get into the habit of doing nothing but studying in your study place and will be able to get to work as soon as you sit down.

READING THE MATERIAL

Some students believe that effective study means to "read the chapter" three or four times. This could be called the "osmosis approach" to studying. You expose yourself to the words in the text and hope something will sink in—like getting a sun tan. This approach does *not* work.

If you just "read the chapter," you'll often realize you've been looking at words but have no idea what they mean. If you come to a difficult idea, you're likely to skip over it. When you reread the chapter, you're likely to recall that the idea was difficult and skip over it again. The result is that you end up having read the chapter three or four times without understanding most of it.

Instead, use an active study technique like the SQ4R system described earlier. Research indicates that active study techniques can dramatically increase how quickly you learn material and how much of it you recall.

UNDERLINING THE TEXT

Many students underline (or highlight) their texts. Underlining works well—but only sometimes. For most people, underlining is not as efficient as taking notes. The danger in underlining is that you tend to underline things to be learned later rather than learning them now. Thus, you can end up with half the chapter underlined and none of it learned. If you *must* underline, try to underline as few words as possible, in the same way as the "key words" approach described in the "Write" section earlier. Avoid used textbooks that someone else has already underlined. They may have been a poor underliner. More importantly, the value of underlining (like the value of taking notes) is in doing it yourself and in learning what's important in the process.

READING SPEED

Slow reading can lead to a number of problems. Most obviously, it takes too long to get through the material. More importantly, you lose interest before you get to the main point. You forget the first part of an idea before you get to the end. (You "lose the forest for the trees.") You may not understand a concept unless it's clearly stated in one sentence. You may misinterpret material because you take so long getting through it that you start reading in your own ideas.

If this description sounds familiar, you might want to check your reading speed. To check your speed, time yourself while you read for exactly five minutes. Estimate the total words you've read and divide by five. To estimate the total words you read, count the number of words in five lines and divide by five (to get the average number of words per line). Then count the number of lines you read and multiply by the number of words per line.

For textbook material, an efficient reading speed is about 350 to 400 words per minute, depending on the difficulty of the topic and your familiarity with it. For novels and other leisure reading, many students can read 600 to 800 words per minute, and "speed readers" can read much faster. Remember that understanding and flexibility in your reading style is more important than mere speed. But often, increased speed actually improves your understanding.

You can increase your reading speed to some extent by conscious effort. If you watch someone read, you'll notice that their eyes move in "jerks" across the line. Our eyes can read words only when stopped. We read a group of words, move our eyes, read the next group, and so on. To increase reading speed, try to take in more words with each eye stop. Don't be concerned with every "and" or "but." Try to notice only words that carry meaning. Read for ideas, not words.

If you read very slowly, you should consider seeking special help. Most campuses have reading laboratories where you can get instruction in increasing your reading speed. Ask your instructor or advisor if your school offers such help.

ANALYZING TESTS

Perhaps you studied hard but still did poorly on the test. How can you make sure the same thing doesn't happen again?

You'll find it helpful to analyze what went wrong on each question you missed. You may be able to do this in class or you may need to see your instructor individually.

Compare the test and your study notes or Study Guide answers. Examine each question you got wrong and reconstruct what happened. For example, did you have the answer in your notes? If so, why didn't you recognize it on the test? Do this for each question you got wrong and look for a pattern. Here are some possibilities.

Was the answer not in your study notes at all? Perhaps you didn't answer all of a study question or otherwise missed important concepts. Perhaps you should talk to your instructor about his or her orientation to the course. What concepts or areas does he or she consider important? What does the instructor want you to learn? Ask the instructor to review your notes and point out where you omitted things he or she considers important.

If your study notes seem complete, go back and compare them to the text. Perhaps you misread the text, got the concept wrong, or only got part of it. Make sure you read the entire section of the text. Sometimes the first sentence of a paragraph only *seems* to convey the idea. Later sentences (or paragraphs) may really convey the core idea. Perhaps, also, you need to read faster. Slow readers often have trouble with complex concepts that aren't clearly stated in one sentence.

Perhaps the answer was in your study notes but you didn't remember it on the test. You can be pleased that you had it in your notes—but why didn't you remember it? Were you too tense? Do you need to recite and review more?

Perhaps you knew the answer but didn't recognize it because of the way the question was phrased. That suggests you're stressing memorization too much. Try to review with someone else. Get them to make you explain your answers and discuss ways they would say it differently. This will help you understand ideas when they are stated differently.

MORE HELP

Many schools have a learning lab or learning skills centre where you can get individualized help. Ask your instructor what facilities your school provides.

For ideas on using the time log below, see "Finding the Time," page ix.

TIME LOG

Date _____

Time	Doing what?	Where?	Comments
7:00 -	-	-	
7:30 -	-	-	
8:00 -	-	-	
8:30 -	-	-	
9:00 -	-	-	
9:30 -	-	-	
10:00 -	-	-	
10:30 -	-	-	
11:00 -	-	-	
11:30 -	-	-	
12:00 -	-	-	
12:30 -	-	-	
1:00 -	-	-	
1:30 -	-	-	
2:00 -	-	-	
2:30 -	-	-	
3:00 -	-	-	
3:30 -	-	-	
4:00 -	-	-	
4:30 -	-	-	
5:00 -	-	-	
5:30 -	-	-	
6:00 -	-	-	
6:30 -	-	-	

Time	Doing what?	Where?	Comments
7:00 -	-	-	
7:30 -	-	-	
8:00 -	-	-	
8:30 -	-	-	
9:00 -	-	-	
9:30 -	-	-	
10:00 -	-	-	
10:30 -	-	-	
11:00 -	-	-	
11:30 -	-	-	
12:00 -	-	-	

Chapter 1

Introduction: Definitional and Historical Considerations and Canada's Mental Health System

OVERVIEW

The first five chapters cover basic ideas and issues in abnormal psychology. These chapters are the background for the rest of the text, which covers the various forms of psychopathology and related topics.

The first two chapters discuss viewpoints on the nature of psychopathology. For example, should people with psychological problems be viewed as "sick," as having "adjustment problems," or as the victims of faulty socialization or learning?

The way we view these problems becomes especially important when discussing ways of classifying and studying psychopathology, which are covered in Chapters 3, 4, and 5. For example, if we view people with these problems as being "mentally ill," then we would want to focus on the illness and developing ways to study, diagnose, and treat it. If, instead, we perceive these people as having learned ineffective behaviours, then we will want to categorize and treat their behaviour differently.

This edition adds information about Canadian society, institutions, the legal system, and the state of abnormal psychology. For some topics, such as the legal system, new sections have been written, and the discussion of the American legal system has been shortened. For other topics, such as the mental health and health care systems, a comparison between the two has been added. Canadian students will find this edition to be relevant to their institutions and will find more overlap with other courses, such as criminology or nursing, where knowledge of Canadian methods and institutions is necessary.

CHAPTER SUMMARY

Chapter 1 covers three major topics.

What Is Abnormal Behaviour? offers five characteristics of abnormality. By themselves, none are adequate definitions of abnormality, but together they provide a framework for understanding it.

The History of Psychopathology shows that different historical periods have emphasized one of three views concerning the causes of psychopathology: demonology (caused by evil outside forces), somatogenesis (bodily causes), or psychogenesis (psychological or mental causes). These three views have led society to view and treat disturbed individuals in very different ways.

Attitudes Toward People with Psychological Disorders discusses the history of societal attitudes towards individuals with mental illnesses and traces the evolution of Canadian institutions that have helped shape a more compassionate attitude toward this population. The twentieth century in Canada saw the rise of large mental institutions and then the reduction in their size, as chemotherapy aided with symptom reduction and community mental health care evolved. This section highlights the work of Clarence Hincks and the Canadian Mental Health Association.

Societies have different fundamental beliefs, values, and social institutions. Canada has developed a health and mental health care system that is universally available and funded by taxes. Because of these values and the resulting social institution of Canada's medicare system, mental patients have access to a relatively advanced level of care. In addition, Canada spends at relatively high rates in both treatment and prevention, which is reflected in higher levels of physical and mental health compared to other countries, such as the United States, where smaller amounts of public money are spent on mental health. Canada is at a critical juncture and in the process of looking at its current health care system and planning for the future through the Commission on the Future of Health Care in Canada.

ESSENTIAL CONCEPTS

1. Abnormality can be characterized in various ways. None of the characteristics hold up perfectly but, together, they provide a framework for understanding abnormality.

2. Throughout history, there have been differing views on the cause of abnormal behaviour. Generally abnormal behaviour has been attributed to outside forces (demonology), bodily factors (somatogenesis), or mental factors (psychogenesis).

3. Contemporary views are based largely on the somatogenic and the psychogenic viewpoints in interaction.

4. The way different societies understand abnormal behaviour strongly affects the way they treat it.

5. Past methods of treating abnormal behaviour have varied and have often been inhumane. However, they may not have been as bad as portrayed, nor are current practices as enlightened as sometimes depicted.

6. Attitudes toward mental illnesses influence the type of treatment and preventative measures supported by society. The evolution of Canadian attitudes in the twentieth century was influenced by the work of the Canadian Mental Health Association.

7. Canada is at a critical juncture with regards to its health care system. Both physical and mental health programs and facilities have been publicly funded since 1970. There is considerable pressure on the federal government to alter this system. The Commission on the Future of Health Care in Canada has made recommendations for changes, and political forces will eventually shape the future of the system.

Route of AB explanation → Demonology
↓
Somato/Psycho
Demonology (13th century)

KEY TERMS

abnormal behaviour (p. 3)

all 5 charecteristics

asylums (p. 9)

accountability (p. 29)

bedlam (p. 9)

best practice models (p. 26)

Canadian Mental Health Association (p. 21)

cathartic method (p. 18)

clinical psychologist (p. 5) *- study abnormal*
- provide diagnosis behaviour
- assessment/evaluation
- research
clinicians (p. 5)
- authorized to provide psychological services

community psychology (p. 27)

community treatment orders (p. 16)

counselling psychologists (p. 6)

deinstitutionalization (p. 25)

demonology (p. 6)
belief that the devil is dwelling in the person and controlling his/her mind and body
diagnosis (p. 5)
learn skills to determine that a patients symptom/problem indicates a disorder.
dissociative identity disorder (p. 21)

evidence-based treatment (p. 26)

exorcism (p. 6)
- since it was thought AB was caused by possession this was done to cast out the evil spirits.

general paresis (p. 17)

germ theory (of disease) (p. 17)

medicare (p. 24)

mental health status (p. 24)

moral treatment (p. 10)

normal curve (p. 3)
- bell shaped curve
- places majority of people in the middle as far as any charecteristic is concerned.
prevention (p. 27)

provincial psychiatric hospitals (p. 15)

psychiatric nurse (p. 6)

psychiatrist (p. 6)
- prescribe psychoactive drugs
- physical examinations
- diagnosing medical problems.
psychoactive drugs (p. 6)

psychoanalyst (p. 6)

psychogenesis (p. 7) *(Rogers, Freud)*
- belief that any form of disturbance in actions/thoughts were due to the mind.
psychopathology (p. 2)
study of the reasons as to why abnormal, thoughts feelings/actions occur.

psychotherapy (p. 5)

*verbal means of helping
a troubled individual
change their thoughts/feelings
and behaviours.*

schizophrenia (p. 21)

stereotyping (p. 20)

stigmatization (p. 20)

social worker (p. 6)

syndrome (p. 16)

somatogenesis (p. 7)

*— introduced by Hippocrates
— believed that disturbances
in the soma (body) were
responsible for disturbances in
thoughts/actions.*

trepanning (p. 6)

*— practice in the stone age/
neolithic era
— creating an opening in the
skull through which evil
spirits can escape.
— DAMAGE to the (upper central
occipital lobe)*

STUDY QUESTIONS

WHAT IS ABNORMAL BEHAVIOUR? (p. 3)

1. Briefly describe five characteristics of abnormality. Explain the strengths and weaknesses of each in defining abnormality. Explain how these characteristics collectively form a framework for understanding abnormality.

Statistical infrequency → *W: base rate for behaviours that are abnormal*   *S: can be used to an extent such as diagnosing mental retardation against normal curve.*
violation of social norms → *behaviours that are deviant such as good athletes*
unexpectedness → *S: some behaviours are socially unacceptable which helps us to categorize as abnormal*   *W: cultural difference as to what is a social norm or not.*
disability/dysfunction
personal distress → *S: behaviour or pattern is hindering the person from functioning normally*   *W: some behaviours don't cause individual any personal distress such as psychopaths.*

HISTORY OF PSYCHOPATHOLOGY (p. 6)

2. Describe demonology and somatogenesis as early theories of the causes of deviant behaviour. How did each explain abnormality? What kinds of treatment resulted from these explanations? (p. 6)

demonology → *the belief that abnormal behaviour such as hallucinations was caused by evil spirits in the head.*

Somatogenesis → *Hippocrates
— belief that disturbances in the body are attributed to disturbed thoughts and actions.
Treatment* → *witchcraft/death/asylums.*

3. Describe an early operation on the human skull performed in Neolithic times. What are two possible reasons why this surgery was done by early Aboriginal peoples in what is now Canada? (p. 6)

Trepanning

Why → *as a way to cure diseases such (associated w/demons) as epilepsy or treat fractures in the skull caused from war.*

4. According to many historians, how did views and treatment of mental illness change during the Dark Ages and change again starting in the thirteenth century? What evidence suggests that the mentally ill were considered witches, and what evidence suggests they were not? (p. 8)

5. Describe the development of asylums for the mentally ill during the fifteenth and sixteenth centuries. How were the mentally ill treated in these early asylums? (p. 9)

> ° They were treated very inhumanely. Treated like zoo animals.

6. Describe the development of moral treatment under Pinel and others. How did this approach view and treat mental illness? Why was this approach largely abandoned? (p. 10)

7. Describe the development of mental health facilities in nineteenth-century Canada. How did this process differ from and how was it similar to the parallel processes in the United States? (p. 11)

8. Describe the development of contemporary views of somatogenesis and psychogenesis. Include the contributions of Kraepelin, Pasteur, Mesmer, Charcot, and Breuer. (p. 17)

CURRENT ATTITUDES TOWARD PEOPLE WITH PSYCHOLOGICAL DISORDERS (p. 20)

9. What are the most important current trends in the institutional care of individuals diagnosed with a mental disorder in Canada? (p. 21)

10. Describe the origins and some important contributions of the Canadian Mental Health Association (CMHA). (p. 22)

11. Compare and contrast the Canadian health care system with that of the United States. (p. 23)

12. Describe the use of "evidence-based treatment" programs. (p. 26)

SELF-TEST, CHAPTER 1

(* Items not covered in Study Questions.)

MULTIPLE CHOICE

1. An example of abnormal behaviour would be
   a. soiling oneself once a month at age 14.
   b. experiencing anxiety and engaging in rituals whenever leaving the house.
   c. losing control of oneself in anger, with no apparent provocation.
   d. all of the above.

2. Which of the following facts highlights a difficulty in defining abnormal behaviour as behaviour that is statistically infrequent?
   a. IQ below 70 is considered mentally retarded.
   b. It is unusual for people to have delusions.
   c. Math prodigies are rare in the population.
   d. Bedwetting is common in young children.

*3. Only psychiatrists can   ⟶ *practicing clinicians*
   a. diagnose mental illness.
   b. conduct research.
   c. conduct psychotherapy.
   d. prescribe medication.

4. Demonology was or is
   a. the practice of exorcism.
   b. devil worship and satanic cults that some viewed as causes of mental illness.
   c. the idea that an evil being may live in a person and control his or her mind and body.
   d. the somatogenic hypothesis of mental illness.

5. The *Malleus Maleficarum* was
   a. a witch hunt manual.
   b. a ceremonial guide used by witches.
   c. a treatment manual used in early mental hospitals.
   d. a Freudian perspective on mental illness.

6. Treatment for the mentally ill became more humane when
   a. moral treatment was introduced.
   b. asylums were abolished.
   c. abnormal behaviour was seen as based upon medical problems.
   d. specialty hospital wards were created for the mentally ill within general care facilities.

7. The early classification system developed by Kraepelin
   a. was based on the psychogenic hypothesis.
   b. was not influential in later diagnostic manuals.

c.   emphasized the continuity of mental illness from normal to abnormal.

d.   assumed each disorder was a distinct entity.

8.   When a group of symptoms typically co-occur, they are called

a.   syndromes.

b.   mental disorders.

c.   diagnoses.

d.   clusters.

9.   Ivy experienced paralysis in her left arm, but there was no neurological basis for her symptoms. This is an illustration of

a.   psychogenic fugue.

b.   hysteria.

c.   post-traumatic stress disorder.

d.   panic disorder.

10.   In contrast to the situation in the United States, the Canadian health care system

a.   does not pay for medical costs of mental patients.

b.   pays the basic medical expenses of mental patients.

c.   was done away with in the 1990s.

d.   pays for medical costs only for the poorest Canadian mental patients.

11.   The Canadian Mental Health Association

a.   had as a co-founder someone who had experienced a mental illness.

b.   had as one of its initial goals assistance for WWI veterans.

c.   focuses on mental illness and mental retardation.

d.   all of the above.

e.   none of the above.

12.   The work of the Canadian Mental Health Association has demonstrated that

a.   people's attitudes toward individuals with mental illness can significantly affect the course of the disease.

b.   lack of public funding can be overcome by volunteer agencies in the care of the mentally ill.

c.   mental patients with public advocates spend less time in prisons than those without.

d.   all of the above.

e.   none of the above.

SHORT ANSWER

1.   What is a limitation of defining abnormality as violation of norms?   • norms are different across cultures.
      Some types of behaviours do not violate any norms that threatens or makes others anxious.

2.   What kinds of treatments evolved from early demonology?
      Exorcism → driving out spirits through prayers/torture.

3. Hippocrates argued that deviant behaviour was not punishment by the gods but a result of . . .

   Some disturbance with the soma (body) that was causing disturbances in behaviour/thought.

4. What evidence suggests that most "witches" were not mentally ill?

   — What the witches claimed they did with satan or what they saw was made to say from torture

5. How were the mentally ill treated in early asylums?

   — no moral treatment — became a
   — made them work   attraction for the
   — confined with lepers   amusement

6. Why was moral treatment largely abandoned?

7. Describe two common misconceptions or myths of mental illness.

   A) unstable/dangerous individuals
   B) Psychological disorders = no cure

8. Describe the work of C.M. Hincks and the CMHA.

9. Describe one contribution of the CMHA that is not viewed in a positive light now.

10. What did the Roland (1990) report on mental institutions in Manitoba find?

11. Describe several attitudes toward people with psychological disorders that are a problem in Canada today.

12. Summarize two of the key recommendations of the Commission on the Future of Health Care in Canada.

ANSWERS TO SELF-TEST, CHAPTER 1

MULTIPLE CHOICE

1. d (p. 3)	2. c (p. 3)	3. d (p. 5)	4. c (p. 6)
5. a (p. 8)	6. a (p. 10)	7. d (p. 16)	8. a (p. 16)
9. b (p. 18)	10. b (p. 23)	11. d (p. 23)	12. a (p. 23)

SHORT ANSWER

1. People with some problems (like anxiety) do not appear different. Also norms vary across cultures. (p. 4)

2. Attempts to induce the demons to leave through prayer, drive them out through torture, etc. (p. 6)

3. ...natural causes. (p. 7)

4. Apparent "hallucinations" of witches were extracted under torture. Government and hospitals recognized and provided for mentally ill. (p. 8)

5. They were confined with lepers and social outcasts under poor conditions. Some asylums sold tickets to people who found their behaviour entertaining. (p. 9)

6. Public hospitals became too large to provide individual care. Physicians gained control and shifted focus to biological factors. (p. 10)

7. Many people believe that people with psychological disorders are unstable and dangerous. Others believe that people with psychological disorders can never be "cured." (p. 20)

8. Between WWI and the present, the CMHA has worked to improve the treatment and prevention programs for mental patients in Canada. Their focus has been on self-help for patients, community education and governmental lobbying. (p. 22)

9. The CNCMH, the precursor organization of the CMHA, supported the involuntary sterilization policies of the Canadian government under the Sexual Sterilization Act of 1928. (p. 23)

10. The Roland report found very difficult and often harsh conditions in mental health facilities across the province and a variety of cases of misdiagnosis and inappropriate placement and treatment. (p. 22)

11. Many Canadians still engage in negative stereotyping and stigmatization and hold beliefs that most mental patients are violent, dangerous, and incurable. (p. 20–21)

12. The Commission on the Future of Health Care in Canada recommended that mental health be made a priority within the system. Specific recommendations included broadening medicare to include a limited number of home-care services and some drug treatments. (p. 28)

2 Current Paradigms and the Role of Cultural Factors

OVERVIEW

This is the second of five introductory chapters covering topics that are basic to the rest of the text. Chapter 1 discussed the role of paradigms in science generally and traced the paradigms that have been important in the history of psychopathology. Many of the differences underlying those paradigms remain unresolved. In particular, the relationship between physical and psychological factors in pathology is still widely debated. As the field has developed, other distinctions have also emerged. These distinctions frame the current paradigms that are described in Chapter 2. You can use these current paradigms to understand and study the various types of psychopathology described later in the text. In addition, Chapter 2 focuses on cultural considerations with an emphasis on Canadian culture, the special situation of Aboriginal peoples, and the Canadian health care system.

Chapters 3 and 4 deal with the topics of classification and assessment. They describe the current categories of psychopathology and the methods used to assess individuals who may have psychological problems. Several issues and controversies are involved in both classifying pathology and assessing individuals. Not surprisingly, these issues are related to differences among the various paradigms presented in Chapters 1 and 2.

Chapter 5 discusses research methods in psychopathology. After Chapter 5, the text begins covering the major forms of abnormality.

CHAPTER SUMMARY

Chapter 2 describes five current paradigms: the biological, psychoanalytic, humanistic/existential, learning, and cognitive paradigms. Each paradigm is a viewpoint or set of assumptions about how to understand, study, and treat psychopathology. As a science matures, there is a tendency for several paradigms to combine into a single, more sophisticated, paradigm. There is some evidence that this process is happening in psychology and psychopathology.

The Biological Paradigm assumes that psychopathology, like medical disease, results from organic factors and that mental states can be understood by understanding the nature of the brain, which produces them. It has led to research into behaviour genetics and brain biochemistry. Biological treatments may have little relation to knowledge about biological factors in the disorder because these are not well enough understood yet, though progress in this field is beginning to accelerate. The biological paradigm can also lead to reductionistic distortions if a practitioner loses sight of how many factors interact to cause a given disorder or symptom.

The Psychoanalytic Paradigm originated with Sigmund Freud who looked for psychological origins of psychopathology in repressed or unconscious processes originating in childhood conflicts. From this perspective, psychoanalytic techniques can help lift the repression so that, as adults, people can face and handle the conflicts. Neo-Freudian analysts have shifted the emphasis from Freud's drive-based views to more interpersonal ones and have developed briefer therapies. Although criticized for lack of scientific evidence to support their claims, Freud's ideas underlie many contemporary ideas in abnormal psychology.

Humanistic and Existential Paradigms also promote insight but focus on the individual person and on the choices that person can and must make in life. Humanistic therapy assumes people make good, growth-enhancing choices when they feel accepted and valued. Existential therapy stresses the inherent anxiety of making choices and accepting their consequences. Gestalt therapy fosters awareness of the immediate here-and-now in which choices are inevitably made.

Learning Paradigms reject mentalistic approaches and view psychopathology as ineffective behaviour acquired through principles of classical conditioning, operant conditioning, and/or modelling. Mediational approaches extend learning principles to internal processes such as anxiety. These approaches have led to more precise methods of studying pathology and to improved treatments. Practitioners of these methods have used the scientific method to test their assumptions and the effectiveness of their techniques.

The Cognitive Paradigm considers a more complex view of learning, emphasizing that individuals actively integrate and interpret new experiences in terms of their existing understandings. Psychopathology is viewed in terms of ineffective understandings or irrational beliefs that may be unlearned and replaced by more rational beliefs. This paradigm has led to popular, effective treatment methods. Cognitive therapists share many beliefs and techniques with behavioural therapists, including a willingness to test theories and methods.

The Consequences of Adopting a Paradigm both focus and limit the search for answers. The *Diathesis-stress* and *Biopsychosocial Models* are *Integrative Paradigms* that combine various viewpoints by considering multiple physical and psychological predispositions (diatheses) to react abnormally to particular environmental stress. The biopsychosocial model looks for complex interactions of biological, psychological, and social forces.

Different Perspectives on a Clinical Problem illustrates how the same problem can make sense from a variety of paradigms. *Eclecticism in Psychotherapy* is a common practice, as therapists adjust their treatments based on a variety of paradigms. Finally, the effects of *Cultural Considerations* are examined with a special focus on the impact of Canada's multiculturalism.

ESSENTIAL CONCEPTS

1. Currently, there are five major paradigms (sets of assumptions) for understanding psychopathology. Each paradigm has developed characteristic terminology, research, and therapeutic approaches.

2. The biological paradigm assumes that the roots of human experience, consciousness, and psychopathology are somatic or bodily in nature, due to the functioning of the brain. This paradigm has produced extensive research on behaviour genetics and brain biochemistry. Psychoactive drugs are used to alter functioning, although their use may not be based on knowledge about causes of the problem. In practice, biological therapists usually try a variety of drugs until one provides symptom relief. This is due to the limited understanding of the actual causes of psychopathology. The paradigm risks over-emphasizing reductionistic assumptions—that behaviour should be understood in terms of "basic" or "underlying" biological factors.

3. The psychoanalytic paradigm assumes that psychopathology results from unconscious or repressed conflicts. Several variations have developed based on Freud's ideas about the structure of the mind, psychosexual stages of development, anxiety, and defences. Psychoanalysts seek to lift repression through various methods, such as dream interpretation, designed to uncover the repressed traumas so that people can deal directly with conflicts.

4.   Humanistic and existential paradigms assume that people can develop and change when they feel valued and supported. These therapists attempt to provide conditions in which clients can make their own choices.

5.   Learning paradigms assert that abnormal behaviour is learned much as normal behaviour is learned. Three major learning processes have emerged: classical conditioning, operant conditioning, and mediational learning. These same processes can be used to change behaviour.

6.   The cognitive paradigm views people as active learners who understand their current experiences in relation to their existing cognitions. Ineffective cognitions can lead to pathology. Drawing out an individual's negative assumptions through discussion and pointing out the destructive nature of those assumptions is one popular therapy. The learning and cognitive paradigms often overlap in practice.

7.   The diathesis-stress paradigm is an attempt to integrate these paradigms. Another paradigm that attempts to understand complex interactions between several variables is the biopsychosocial model. Both of these draw on valid concepts from all other paradigms and combine them into a more comprehensive, integrated paradigm.

8.   In practice, most therapists arc cclectic, blending elements from various paradigms to individualize treatment.

9.   There are unique issues relative to psychopathology and social policy for a multicultural society like Canada. For example, almost all cultures have types of psychopathology that are unique to that cultural group.

10.   Canada's Aboriginal communities face unique mental health challenges due to their cultural history and current economic and geographical circumstances. Many groups are attempting to reassert their traditional methods of dealing with mental health issues.

KEY TERMS

acculturation (p. 69)   behaviour genetics (p. 34)

action therapies (p. 43)   behaviour modification (p. 54)

adoptees method (p. 35)   behaviour rehearsal (p. 62)

assertion training (p. 56)   behaviour therapy (p. 54)

assimilation (p. 69)   behaviourism (p. 50)

aversive conditioning (p. 54)   biological paradigm (p. 33) biopsychosocial paradigm (p. 64)

constructivist-narrative approach (p. 60)

brain stem (p. 38)

corpus callosum (p. 37)

brief therapy (p. 44)

counterconditioning (p. 54)

cerebellum (p. 39)

countertransference (p. 42)

cerebral cortex (p. 37)

cultural diversity (p. 68)

cerebral hemispheres (p. 37)

defence mechanism (p. 41)

classical conditioning (p. 50)

denial (p. 41)

client-centred therapy (p. 46)

diathesis–stress paradigm (p. 63)

cognition (p. 57)

diencephalon (p. 38)

cognitive behaviour therapy (CBT) (p. 58)

discriminative stimulus (p. 51)

cognitive paradigm (p. 57)

disease model (p. 33)

cognitive restructuring (p. 58)

displacement (p. 41)

concordance (p. 34)

dizygotic (DZ) twins (p. 34)

conditioned response (p. 51)

dream analysis (p. 42)

conditioned stimulus (p. 51)

eclecticism (p. 62)

ego (p. 41)

instrumental learning (p. 51)

ego analysis (p. 43)

interpersonal therapy (IPT) (p. 45)

extinction (p. 51)

interpretation (p. 42)

family method (p. 34)

introspection (p. 50)

free association (p. 42)

irrational beliefs (p. 58)

frontal lobe (p. 37)

latent content (p. 42)

genes (p. 34)

law of effect (p. 51)

genotype (p. 34)

learning (or behavioural) paradigm (p. 50)

Gestalt therapy (p. 48)

libido (p. 40)

gyri (p. 37)

limbic system (p. 39)

humanistic and existential therapies (p. 46)

linkage analysis (p. 35)

hypothalamus (p. 38)

mediational theory of learning (p. 53)

id (p. 40)

mediator (p. 53)

index cases (probands) (p. 34)

medical model (p. 33)

insight therapies (p. 43)

medulla oblongata (p. 38)

meninges (p. 37)

midbrain (p. 38)

modelling (p. 52)

monozygotic (MZ) twins (p. 34)

moral anxiety (p. 41)

multicultural counselling and therapy (p. 68)

negative reinforcement (p. 52)

nerve impulse (p. 36)

neuron (p. 36)

neurotic anxiety (p. 41)

neurotransmitters (p. 36)

nuclei (p. 38)

objective (realistic) anxiety (p. 41)

occipital lobe (p. 38)

Oedipus complex (p. 42)

operant conditioning (p. 51)

paradigm (p. 33)

parietal lobe (p. 37)

phenotype (p. 34)

pleasure principle (p. 40)

pons (p. 38)

positive reinforcement (p. 52)

primary process thinking (p. 40)

projection (p. 41)

psychoanalytic (psychodynamic) paradigm (p. 40)

psychodynamics (p. 41)

psychotherapy (p. 43)

rational-emotive behaviour therapy (REBT) (p. 58)

rationalization (p. 41)

reaction formation (p. 41)

reality principle (p. 41)

reductionism (p. 40)

regression (p. 41)

repression (p. 41)

resilience (p. 65)

resistance (p. 42)

reticular formation (p. 39)

reuptake (p. 36)

risk (p. 65)

role-playing (p. 45)

schema (p. 57)

secondary process thinking (p. 41)

self-actualization (p. 46)

self-efficacy (p. 53)

self-instructional training (p. 60)

shaping (p. 52)

stress-inoculation training (p. 60)

sublimation (p. 41)

successive approximation (p. 52)

sulci (p. 37)

superego (p. 41)

sympathetic nervous system (p. 36)

synapse (p. 36)

systematic desensitization (p. 54)

temporal lobe (p. 37)

thalamus (p. 38)

time-out (p. 55)   unconditioned response (p. 51)

token economy (p. 55)   unconditioned stimulus (p. 51)

transference (p. 42)   unconscious (p. 40)

twin method (p. 34)   ventricles (p. 38)

unconditional positive regard (p. 47)   white matter (p. 38)

STUDY QUESTIONS

THE ROLE OF PARADIGMS (p. 33)

1. What role do paradigms play in the evolution of science? (p. 33) How is the diathesis-stress model an attempt to integrate several existing paradigms? (p. 63)

2. Discuss the overall goal of the study of molecular genetics and how it might influence future applications to abnormal psychology. (p. 35)

THE BIOLOGICAL PARADIGM (p. 33)

3. What are the assumptions of the biological paradigm? Describe the behaviour genetics view of the relationship between genes and abnormal behaviour. Describe four research methods in behaviour genetics and any limitations of each. (p. 33)

4. Describe the biochemistry of the nervous system, especially neurotransmitters. Identify three neurotransmitter problems that could be linked to psychopathology. (p. 36)

5.   Briefly describe three relationships between treatment and knowledge that a disorder has biological causes. Evaluate the biological paradigm by defining reductionism and the problem with it. (p. 33)

THE PSYCHOANALYTIC PARADIGM (p. 40)

6.   What is the central assumption of the psychoanalytic paradigm? Briefly describe Freud's classical theory including three mental functions and how they interact. (p. 40)

7.   How does neurotic anxiety develop, according to Freud's earlier and later theories? Describe what is repressed in each theory. How do defense mechanisms minimize anxiety and indicate it exists? (p. 40)

8.   According to psychoanalytic therapy, what can happen once repression is lifted? Describe four techniques and how each helps in reaching the goal of lifting repression. (p. 42)

9.   Identify three modifications of psychoanalytic therapy. Describe the major assumption of each and how therapy methods changed as a result. Evaluate the psychoanalytic paradigm by identifying four criticisms and four contributions. (p. 42)

HUMANISTIC AND EXISTENTIAL PARADIGMS (p. 46)

10.   How are humanistic and existential paradigms similar to and different from psychoanalytic paradigms? Describe five assumptions underlying Carl Rogers' client-centred therapy. Describe three characteristics of Rogers' therapeutic intervention. (p. 46)

11.   Describe three attitudes of existential therapists; look for (a) uncertainties of life, (b) anxiety and choice, (c) accepting responsibility. Describe two goals of existential therapy. Describe the central goal of Gestalt therapy. Describe five Gestalt techniques and how each can help reach the basic goal. (p. 46)

12.   Evaluate humanistic-existential paradigms by describing (a) two criticisms of their assumptions and (b) research on client-centred therapy. (p. 50)

LEARNING PARADIGMS (p. 50)

13.   How did dissatisfaction with introspection lead to the rise of the learning paradigm? What are the assumptions of behaviourism as developed by Watson and others? Describe three conditioning models (classical, operant, and modelling) which developed out of behavioural assumptions. How did mediational learning paradigms modify behavioural assumptions? How did this modification expand the field? (p. 50)

14.   Describe the difference between other learning paradigms and Bandura's observational learning. (p. 52)

15.   Behaviour therapy is characterized by what general approach? Briefly describe an example of a behaviour therapy that developed out of each of the three conditioning models. Evaluate learning paradigms by describing two issues. (p. 50)

THE COGNITIVE PARADIGM (p. 57)

16.   What is the basic assumption of the cognitive paradigm (especially that cognition is "active")? How does past knowledge influence learning of new information? Describe the cognitive behaviour therapy approaches of Ellis and of Beck. Evaluate the cognitive paradigm by discussing two basic issues. Describe the contributions to the cognitive paradigm by Canadian Donald Meichenbaum. (p. 57)

CONSEQUENCES OF ADOPTING A PARADIGM/ECLECTICISM (p. 61)

17.   How do paradigms have consequences for the ways researchers collect and interpret data? Describe the diathesis-stress and biopsychosocial paradigms as ways to make current paradigms more flexible. What are three key points of these approaches? Finally, what does it mean to say that eclecticism in psychotherapy is common? (p. 61)

18.   What unique challenges are faced in Canada, due to its multiculturalism, in the areas of social policy and research in the field of abnormal psychology? (p. 68)

19.   Describe the problems faced by Canada's Aboriginal peoples and their attempts to rekindle their traditional methods of treating and preventing mental illness. (p. 68)

SELF-TEST, CHAPTER 2

(* Items not covered in the Study Questions.)

MULTIPLE CHOICE   — scientific perspective (set of rules/guidelines)

1.   The basic role of a paradigm in scientific research is to
   a.   provide funding for scientific research projects.
   b.   set the ethical standards for the conduct of scientific research.
   c.   specify what problems scientists in a given field will research.
   d.   set an example for younger researchers in a scientific field of study.

2.   Bandura's more recent work is a cognitive self-regulation theory known as social cognitive theory, which focuses on the concept of human agency and
   a.   self efficacy.
   b.   the administration of electric shock.
   c.   drug treatments.
   d.   frontal lobotomy.

3.   Neurotransmitters

    a.   deliver nerve impulse information between neurons.

    b.   allow for the detection of brain activity, through measures such as EEG.

    c.   transmit genetic information from parents to offspring. ✗

    d.   block the flow of information and contribute to behavioural problems.

4.   The psychoanalytic paradigm rests upon the assumption that psychopathology is the result of

    a.   incomplete superego development.

    b.   unconscious conflicts.

    c.   ego defence mechanisms.

    d.   a breakdown of control over the pleasure principle.

5.   According to Freud, fixation at a particular stage results in

    a.   difficulties in determining the nature of the conflicts when the person enters analysis.

    b.   a sexually unresponsive individual.

    c.   an inability to develop further.

    d.   regression to that stage when stressed later in life.

6.   Defence mechanisms are produced by the _____, which is in the _____.

    a.   ego; unconscious

    b.   superego; unconscious   *defence*
                                                    mechanism

    c.   id; preconscious

    d.   ego; conscious

                                      ~ Roger (self-actualization)

7.   A major emphasis of client-centred therapy is *– empathy*

                                           – UPR

    a.   emphasizing self-actualization.

    b.   unconditional positive regard.

    c.   to improve awareness of one's own behaviour.

    d.   all of the above.

8.   As part of the behaviourism movement in psychology, there was a movement away from _____ techniques, and a movement toward _____ techniques for studying behaviour.

    a.   the case study; correlational studies

    b.   phenomenology; operant conditioning

    c.   introspection; direct observation

    d.   determinism; the concept of free will

9.   When you attempt to buy a soda from a machine, you only do so if the lights are on. According to Skinner, the lights on the soda machine are   *discriminative⇒*

    a.   positive reinforcement.   *something in the*
                                                    environment that tells u
    b.   a discriminative stimulus.   *if you were to produce a*
                                                    response. the consequence
    c.   a signal for extinction.   *that will occur.*

    d.   a conditioned stimulus.

10.   Which paradigm argues that people interpret events selectively and experience emotions based upon those interpretations?
    a.   psychoanalytic paradigm ✗
    b.   cognitive paradigm
    c.   learning paradigm
    d.   diathesis-stress paradigm ✗

11.   The diathesis-stress paradigm emphasizes that abnormality results from
    a.   biological factors and the unconscious.
    b.   predisposition and current pressures.
    c.   physiology and biochemistry.
    d.   attachment and Gestalt problems.

12.   Contemporary psychologists primarily consider themselves
    a.   eclectic.   → multidisciplinary
    b.   psychoanalytic or psychodynamic therapists.
    c.   behaviour therapists.
    d.   cognitive or cognitive-behaviour therapists.

13.   The American model of cultural assimilation or "melting pot" can be contrasted with the Canadian model of preserving minority cultures known as
    a.   cultural mosaic.
    b.   cultural preservation.
    c.   cultural diversification.
    d.   Aboriginal acculturation.

14.   Which dimension is not suggested as a potential grouping variable for diversity by the textbook?
    a.   language
    b.   race
    c.   region of birth
    d.   visible racial differences

~ predisposition

15.   A possible "diathesis" for schizophrenia would be
    a.   "schizophrenegenic" mothers
    b.   a genetic predisposition
    c.   adolescent stress
    d.   all of the above
    e.   none of the above

16.   Which group has been observed to seek help from mental health professionals at a lower rate than other groups?
    a.   First Nations
    b.   Europeans
    c.   Asians
    d.   Latin Americans

SHORT ANSWER

1. Describe an advantage and disadvantage for a field of science guided by a paradigm.

   Advantage → boundaries to follow research

   Disadvantage → bias in data collection

2. According to behavioural genetics, what is the relationship between genes and abnormal behaviour?

   Genes are continually shaped by the environment ⇒ produce the phenotype/behaviour.

3. Why is "reductionism" a problem when developing theories?

   • Because it reduces psychopathology and psychology in general to mostly biological in nature which cannot be done.

4. In psychoanalysis, why is lifting repression desirable?

   Repression ⇒ unresolved conflicts from the past that is causing the abnormal behaviours or not allowing the person to move on.   *By lifting them the individual can move into adult reality.*

5. Identify three lasting contributions of Freud and psychoanalysis.

6. Identify a similarity and a difference between psychoanalysis and humanistic/existential paradigms.

   similarity ⇒ insight therapy (gaining insight into why the patient producing AB

   difference ⇒ psycho ⇒ unconscious/past   H/E ⇒ here and now

7. Summarize the existential view about "choices" in people's lives.

8. Give two criticisms of humanistic approaches to therapy.

9. Behaviour therapy is distinguished by what general approach to abnormality?

10. How would a therapist using Ellis' cognitive behavioural therapy deal with a college student who is anxious over grades?

11. Describe the major advance in cognitive psychotherapy introduced by Donald Meichenbaum.

12. Describe the general nature of the biopsychosocial paradigm for understanding the cause of psychopathology.

13. What factors have contributed to the causes of high rates of mental health problems among Canada's Aboriginal peoples?

14. Describe the two most serious barriers to full utilization of Canadian mental health facilities by Asian Canadians.

ANSWERS TO SELF-TEST, CHAPTER 2

MULTIPLE CHOICE

1. c (p. 33)	2. a (p. 53)	3. a (p. 36)	4. b (p. 40)	5. d (p. 41)
6. a (p. 41)	7. d (p. 46)	8. c (p. 50)	9. b (p. 51)	10. b (p. 57)
11. b (p. 63)	12. a (p. 76)	13. a (p. 69)	14. b (p. 69)	15. b (p. 66)
16. c (p. 69)				

SHORT ANSWER

1. Paradigms provide guidance for researchers by setting the boundaries of what is acceptable in a given field, but they also bias the definitions and methods of data collection. (p. 33)

2. Phenotypes (or observable behaviour characteristics) result from interaction of environment and genotypes (unobservable, genetic influences). (p. 34)

3. Reductionistic explanations could be reduced again and again with no assurance the answers would apply to the original phenomena. (p. 40)

4. By lifting repression, the patient can face the conflict and resolve it in light of adult reality. The patient can recognize what motivates him or her and make better choices. (p. 42)

5. Freud identified the importance of (a) childhood, (b) unconscious influences on behaviour, (c) defence mechanisms, and (d) non-obvious factors in behaviour. (p. 45)

6. They are similar in emphasis on insight and awareness. They are different in seeing human nature as asocial urges needing restraint vs. making choices, goodness, and growth. (p. 46)

7. Living involves anxiety-provoking choices. Growth comes from facing the anxiety and making the choices. (p. 47)

8. (a) It is unclear that a therapist can ever truly understand a client's phenomenological world (b) It is unclear that people are really good and able to solve their own problems. (p. 50)

9. Behaviour therapy requires an epistemological stance of seeking rigorous proof and the application of experimental methods and knowledge. (p. 50)

10. He or she would challenge irrational beliefs about grades such as "I should always make A's" or "If I flunk out that would be terrible." (p. 57)

11. He developed a multi-component coping-skills approach that incorporates self-instructional training that emphasizes systematic acquisition of coping skills through learning to cope with small but manageable amounts of stress. (p. 59)

12. The biopsychosocial paradigm is an attempt to combine several variables. The cause of any mental disorder is seen as the interaction of biological (genetic or environmental), psychological (learning), and social factors (for example, peer pressure) that interact. (p. 63)

13. The unique mental health problems of Canada's Aboriginal peoples has been attributed to 300 years of institutionalized discrimination, attempts at forced cultural assimilation (such at the residential school movement), poverty, and generally poor living conditions. (p. 67)

14. Asian Canadians avoid therapy because of (a) poor English language ability, especially among the Chinese and Indian respondents and (b) a culturally-determined interpretation of psychological disorders that decreases the likelihood of seeking help. (p. 67)

Chapter 3 Classification and Diagnosis

OVERVIEW

This is the third of five introductory chapters. The first two chapters covered historical and contemporary paradigms or theories of abnormality. The remaining three chapters deal with less theoretical issues. Chapter 3 summarizes the standard diagnostic system for classifying disturbed individuals. It also discusses basic issues regarding classification. Chapter 4 deals with issues and methods of assessment. Mental health professionals use these methods for both individual assessment and research. Chapter 5 covers research methods and will complete the introductory chapters.

Chapters 3, 4, and 5 are less overtly theoretical than the earlier chapters. Still, the paradigm differences continue and are reflected in differences about how best to classify and study abnormality.

CHAPTER SUMMARY

Chapter 3 discusses the standard system for categorizing psychopathology and issues concerning this system as well as classification generally.

A Brief History of Classification describes early attempts to categorize abnormality and the development of categories in the current system.

The Diagnostic System of the American Psychiatric Association (DSM-IV) summarizes some general characteristics of the current standard diagnostic system, especially its multiaxial classification approach. The chapter summarizes the main categories in *DSM-IV*. Later chapters cover these categories in detail. A Canadian perspective is presented: it includes a summary of the McGill youth gambling research plus Canadian statistics on the incidence of mental disorders in Canada.

Issues in the Classification of Abnormal Behaviour are (1) whether people should be classified at all and (2) whether *DSM-IV* is a good classification system. Classification loses information and may stigmatize people. However, some classification system is needed in order to study and treat problems. Earlier DSM systems were criticized for lack of reliability (consistency in applying labels) and validity (accuracy of the labels). *DSM-IV* appears more reliable but its broader utility is not yet clear. There are a number of theorists and practitioners who are looking to radically alter the current DSM or replace it completely with a fully dimensional scheme.

ESSENTIAL CONCEPTS

1. Early classification systems did not clearly define disorders and were not widely accepted. Recent DSMs have provided extensive descriptions and clear reasons for label changes, leading to wider acceptance.

2. The organization of mental disorders in the current DSM is the basis for organizing much of the textbook.

3. The current *DSM-IV* is multiaxial, inviting therapists to consider five axes or dimensions when making a diagnosis.

4. In *DSM-IV*, problems are classified in sixteen major categories, which are defined in this chapter.

5. Some critics object to the very concept of classifying abnormal behaviour, because it can cause loss of information and can stigmatize people. However, some system of distinguishing different problems seems needed.

6. DSM has been criticized for using discrete categories rather than dimensions or degrees of abnormality.

7. Earlier DSMs were criticized for low reliability (consistency of diagnosis), which limited their validity or accuracy.

8. *DSM-IV* contains specific diagnostic criteria and, as a result, has proven more reliable than its predecessors. However, its validity is uncertain, and other problems remain.

9. Some professionals recommend that the DSM system be replaced by a fully dimensional system.

KEY TERMS

categorical classification (p. 92)

DSM-IV-TR (p. 79)

comorbidity (p. 90)

epidemiology (p. 86)   *distribution/ frequency*

construct validity (p. 93)

help-seeking (p. 90)

Diagnostic and Statistical Manual of Mental
Disorders (DSM) (p. 79)

inter-rater reliability (p. 93)

dimensional classification (p. 92)

lifetime prevalence (p. 89)

DSM-IV (p. 79)

mental disorder (p. 80)

multiaxial classification (p. 80)   prevalence (p. 86)

pathological gambling (p. 86)   reliability (p. 93)

STUDY QUESTIONS

A BRIEF HISTORY OF CLASSIFICATION (p. 79)

1. What developments in other fields led to early interest in classifying abnormality? What was the problem with early classification systems? Identify two improvements of DSM systems beginning in 1988. (p. 79)

2. What are the five axes in *DSM-IV* and the rationale for distinguishing them (especially axes I and II)? (p. 80)

3. Identify and define the major diagnostic categories involved in axes I and II (16 in all). You may also wish to refer to the glossary in the back of the text. (p. 80)

4. Summarize the effects of the liberalization of gambling laws in the 1980s on mental health in Canada. (p. 85)

5. Describe several findings about the prevalence of psychological disorders from the Ontario Health Survey (1994). (p. 88)

ISSUES IN THE CLASSIFICATION OF ABNORMAL BEHAVIOUR (p. 91)

6.   Summarize two general criticisms of classification and the counter-arguments to each. Despite these criticisms, what is the general value of classification and diagnosis? (p. 91)

7.   Briefly identify three specific criticisms of diagnosis. (p. 91)

8.   For the first criticism in question 6 or 7, distinguish between categorical and dimensional approaches. Give one reason why a dimensional system ought to be an improvement and two reasons why it might not be one. (p. 91)

9.   Define "reliability" and "validity." Explain them as issues in a classification system such as DSM. (p. 93)

10.   Describe three things done to improve the reliability of recent DSMs. (p. 93)

11.   What six problems remain in the DSM system? (p. 94)

12.   What future changes are recommended for the official system of diagnosis? (p. 97)

SELF-TEST, CHAPTER 3

(* Items not covered in the Study Questions.)

MULTIPLE CHOICE

1. In preparing the *DSM-IV*, working groups were formed for different classes of disorders to
    a.   prepare literature reviews regarding disorders.
    b.   collect additional data if necessary.
    c.   analyze old data.
    d.   all of the above.

2. Axes I and II are distinguished
    a.   so acute diagnoses may be emphasized on two axes.
    b.   for greater precision in treatment.
    c.   in order to account for enduring problems.
    d.   to distinguish childhood and adult disorders.

3. John is difficult to understand when he speaks. Specifically, his comments are illogical, and he frequently shows signs of delusional ideas, such as the idea that his thoughts were placed there by someone else. What is the most likely diagnostic category for John based on this information?
    a.   anxiety disorders
    b.   schizophrenia
    c.   dissociative disorders
    d.   somatoform disorders

*4. Multiple personality disorder is just another name for
    a.   schizophrenia.
    b.   dissociative identity disorder.
    c.   dissociative fugue.
    d.   autism.

*5. Why does the DSM-IV include an appendix on diagnostic categories that have not yet been supported by sufficient data?
    a.   To encourage researchers to study them.
    b.   To warn professionals familiar with earlier editions of the DSM not to continue using them.
    c.   To attract media attention.
    d.   To enable professionals to treat individuals not fitting one of the traditional diagnoses.

6. The diagnoses of the DSM are referred to as _____ because they are inferred, not proven, entities. A diagnosis of schizophrenia, for instance, does not have the same status as a diagnosis of diabetes.
    a.   constructs
    b.   hypotheses
    c.   guesses
    d.   projections

7. An alternative to the DSM has been suggested, which bases diagnoses on
    a. exclusively theory-driven criteria.
    b. ratings along quantitative dimensions.
    c. an accumulation of symptoms that describe different diagnostic entities.
    d. None of the above choices have been suggested as alternatives to the DSM.

8. In order to study the reliability of a diagnostic category, therapists would study whether
    a. it acknowledges the uniqueness of each individual.
    b. it has explicitly stated criteria.
    c. patients with the label respond to treatment the same.
    d. diagnosticians apply it consistently.

9. Epidemiology is the study of
    a. the epidermis.
    b. questions of epistemology.
    c. the frequency and distribution of a disorder in a given population.
    d. the causes of mental disorders.

10. Which of the following is not true of findings in Ontario regarding the prevalence of psychological disorders?
    a. Alcohol abuse or dependence is almost four times higher among men than among women.
    b. There is a higher rate of anti-social behaviour in men than in women.
    c. Major depression is more common in women than in men.
    d. The rate is high for both men and women in the age range 15–24.

11. Construct validity of a diagnosis refers to
    a. diagnoses that arise due to known medical factors.
    b. the consistency of diagnosing the same condition.
    c. whether accurate statements and predictions can be made about it.
    d. the likelihood that two diagnosticians would come up with the same diagnosis.

12. People diagnosed with schizophrenia usually respond well to haloperidol, whereas people with anxiety disorders do not. This is evidence for the _____ of the diagnosis of schizophrenia.
    a. reliability
    b. validity
    c. categorical classification
    d. dimensional classification

SHORT ANSWER

1. What was the problem with early classification systems?

2. What are the characteristics of somatoform disorders in *DSM-IV?*

3. Define and give an example of "mood disorders."

4. The two major groups of issues regarding the classification of abnormal behaviour are _____ and _____.

5. One possible criticism of current diagnostic practice is that it is difficult to indicate degrees of abnormality because...

6. Describe methods of helping pathological gamblers.

7. Describe one of the limitations of the Ontario study.

8. A diagnostic label is _____ if diagnosticians agree on applying it to particular individuals.

9. Dr. Jones has just developed the new diagnostic label of "Sprangfordism." How will he demonstrate the construct validity of this label?

10. What has been done to improve the reliability of recent DSMs?

11. In what way are diagnostic decision-making rules not clearly ideal in DSM?

12. What do Watson and Clark suggest as possible forms of the next version of the DSM?

ANSWERS TO SELF-TEST, CHAPTER 3

MULTIPLE CHOICE

1. d (p. 79)	2. c (p. 80)	3. b (p. 83)	4. b (p. 84)
5. a (p. 95)	6. a (p. 93)	7. b (p. 92)	8. d (p. 93)
9. c (p. 86)	10. b (p. 86)	11. c (p. 93)	12. b (p. 93)

SHORT ANSWER

1. They had vague definitions and were not widely accepted. There was no consensus. (p. 79)

2. Physical symptoms that have a psychological, not a medical, cause. (p. 83)

3. Mood disorders are disturbances of mood or affect, such as depression or mania. (p. 83)

4. General criticisms of classification (i.e., whether classification is useful and desirable); criticisms of actual diagnostic practices (i.e., DSM). (p. 91)

5. The labels are discrete categorical entities (i.e., people either are, or are not, labelled). (p. 92)

6. Cognitive-behaviour treatments that target underlying problems such as depression, loss, poor coping skills, and ineffective social skills, along with family involvement, have been shown to be effective. (p. 85)

7. Problems are the exclusion of people over 64 years of age, individuals living in institutions, the homeless, and Aboriginal people. In addition, schizophrenia and related psychotic disorders were not studied. (p. 89)

8. reliable (p. 93)

9. He must show that accurate statements can be made about people who receive the label. For example, they are different from others in their behaviour, background, prognosis, response to treatment, etc. (p. 93)

10. Symptoms and criteria for making a diagnosis were defined more clearly and after considering cultural and other factors. (p. 94)

11. The rules seem arbitrary (why 3 of 6 characteristics rather than 2 or 4 or 6?). They still involve subjective judgements. (p. 94)

12. They suggest that *DSM V* will either be a hybrid, in which at least Axis II will be dimensional, or it will involve multiple systems, with each system designed for different uses. (p. 97)

Chapter 4 Clinical Assessment Procedures

OVERVIEW

This is the fourth of five introductory chapters covering basic issues in psychopathology. The first two chapters cover historical and contemporary paradigms or theories of abnormality. Chapter 3 deals with *DSM-IV*, the standard system for classifying abnormality, and then summarizes general issues regarding classification.

This chapter discusses the major methods used to assess and classify behaviour, as well as issues underlying these methods. Many of these issues concern the accuracy of assessment methods. Other issues involve the paradigms discussed in Chapters 1 and 2.

Chapter 5 covers research methods and completes the introductory chapters. Research issues are included in earlier chapters (and appear throughout the text). Chapter 5 brings these issues together by showing the relative strengths and limitations of various research approaches.

Chapter 6 begins eleven chapters covering the various forms of abnormality. The last two chapters cover related topics in abnormal psychology.

CHAPTER SUMMARY

Chapter 4 describes various methods and issues in assessing individuals and their problems. It discusses issues regarding the accuracy of assessments and describes methods of assessment. Not surprisingly, these methods are based on the various paradigms discussed in earlier chapters.

Reliability and Validity in Assessment describes ways of studying the reliability (or repeatability) and validity (or accuracy) of various approaches to assessment. These concepts are used in evaluating the assessment methods described in this chapter. Generally, reliability precedes validity. That is, techniques that are not reliable or repeatable cannot easily be accurate.

Psychological Assessment covers traditional assessment techniques of clinical interviews and psychological tests (including personality inventories, projective measures, and intelligence tests). It also describes assessment techniques developed out of the behavioural and cognitive paradigms. The McMaster Family Assessment Device is discussed as an example of family assessment in action.

Biological Assessment describes methods of assessing biological influences on behaviour. Brain imaging and neurochemical methods examine the brain itself. Neuropsychological methods examine the effects of brain dysfunction on behaviour. Psychophysiological methods examine bodily changes that accompany behaviour, including changes in sweating, breathing, and heart rate. Although these methods seem precise, they have difficulty accounting for how well individuals may adapt to neurological damage.

The last two sections of the chapter discuss important (and largely unanswered) issues in assessment. *Cultural Diversity and Clinical Assessment* discusses issues in assessing individuals of differing cultures. Studies suggest clinicians may misdiagnose pathology in individuals of other cultures. These studies suggest the need for great sensitivity and awareness of cultural variation. IQ testing with Canadian Aboriginal groups is a specific example of the practical problems encountered by psychometricians in contemporary Canadian society.

The Consistency and Variability of Behaviour reviews a basic argument over whether behaviour is consistent or variable across situations. Traditional paradigms focus on personality traits leading to predictions that behaviour will be consistent across situations. Behavioural paradigms and assessments suspect behaviour varies with the situation.

ESSENTIAL CONCEPTS

1. Assessment methods are evaluated in terms of "reliability" and "validity." Methods must yield reliable or repeatable results before their validity or accuracy can be effectively studied.

2. Traditional psychological assessment methods include clinical interviews, personality inventories, projective techniques, and intelligence tests.

3. Clinical interviews can be useful in establishing rapport. They are often unstructured and results depend on the interviewer's skill, paradigm, etc.

4. Personality tests are standardized, structured self-report measures but are limited by various problems of all self-report data.

5. Projective tests rely on individuals projecting their personality as they respond to ambiguous stimuli. The unstructured nature of these procedures has made them difficult to evaluate.

6. Intelligence tests predict academic potential with some success but can be misused and misinterpreted.

7. Although direct observation is the hallmark of behavioural assessment, self-report and cognitive measures are also used.

8. Family assessment is a specialized field that draws on a variety of theories and methods. Because a family is seen as an evolving system, assessment methods must be dynamic.

9. Biological assessment methods study the brain, behavioural effects of brain dysfunction, and physiological aspects of behaviour. Each method has advantages but can be misinterpreted.

10. Psychologists are becoming aware of issues in assessing individuals from differing cultures. Insensitivity to cultural variation may lead to misdiagnosis.

KEY TERMS

alternate-form reliability (p. 100)

behavioural observation (p. 111)

clinical interview (p. 101)

cognitive-behavioural case formulation (p. 109)

construct validity (p. 101)

content validity (p. 101)

criterion validity (p. 101)

CT scan (p. 118)

cultural bias (p. 125)

ecological momentary assessment (EMA) (p. 112)

electrocardiogram (p. 122)

electrodermal responding (p. 123)

electroencephalogram (EEG) (p. 123)

event-related potential (ERP) (p. 124)

family functioning (p. 115)

functional magnetic resonance imaging (fMRI) (p. 118)

intelligence test (p. 108)

internal consistency reliability (p. 100)

inter-rater reliability (p. 100)

magnetic resonance imaging (MRI) (p. 118)

Minnesota Multiphasic Personality Inventory (MMPI) (p. 104)

neurologist (p. 120)

neuropsychological tests (p. 120)

neuropsychologist (p. 120)

personality inventory (p. 104)

PET scan (p. 119)

projective hypothesis (p. 106)

projective test (p. 106)   standardization (p. 104)

psychological tests (p. 104)   structured interview (p. 101)

psychophysiology (p. 122)   test–retest reliability (p. 100)

reactivity (of behaviour) (p. 113)   Thematic Apperception Test (TAT) (p. 106)

Rorschach Inkblot Test (p. 106)   thought listing (p. 114)

self-monitoring (p. 112)   videotape reconstruction (p. 114)

STUDY QUESTIONS

RELIABILITY AND VALIDITY IN ASSESSMENT (p. 100)

1.   Define reliability and validity and the relationship between them. Briefly describe four types of reliability and three types of validity. (p. 100)

PSYCHOLOGICAL ASSESSMENT (p. 101)

2.   Identify three general approaches to psychological assessment (p. 101). How are interviews similar to and different from normal conversation? Describe how four variables (paradigms, rapport, situational factors, and structure) influence interview results. (p. 102)

3.   Identify three types of psychological tests (p. 104). As an example of personality inventories, what was the MMPI designed to do? How was it developed, and why was it revised? Briefly discuss the issue of faking on the MMPI. (p. 104)

4. What is the assumption underlying projective tests? How have they become more objective over the years? (p. 106)

5. What are intelligence tests designed to predict? What other uses do they have? Evaluate intelligence tests in terms of criterion validity and construct validity. (p. 108)

6. Distinguish between traditional and behavioural/cognitive assessment using the SORC acronym. Describe three approaches to behavioural and cognitive assessment using examples to illustrate the range of techniques. (p. 109)

7. Describe the most important methods used in family assessment, with reference to the theoretical basis for their use. Describe the six stages of the McMaster Family Assessment Device. (p. 115)

BIOLOGICAL ASSESSMENT (p. 118)

8. Describe three approaches to studying nervous system functioning and give examples. Identify advantages and disadvantages of each approach. (p. 118)

9. Describe psychophysiological measurement and give examples. Identify a limitation of this approach. Give two reasons to be cautious about biological assessment procedures generally. (p. 122)

CULTURAL DIVERSITY AND CLINICAL ASSESSMENT (p. 125)

10. What is the basic question regarding cultural diversity and clinical assessment? Give examples of clinicians under- and overpathologizing the problems of individuals from other cultures. What position does the text take on (a) being aware of cultural differences and (b) including cultural differences in assessment? Identify four strategies for avoiding cultural bias in assessment. (p. 125)

11. Describe the efforts to develop valid methods of assessing the IQ of Aboriginal Canadians. (p. 126)

SELF-TEST, CHAPTER 4

(* Items not covered in the Study Questions.)

MULTIPLE CHOICE

1. Diane is taking a personality test. The test has items that are all closely related to one another. This is an example of
   a. external validity.
   b. internal consistency.
   c. internal validity.
   d. test-retest reliability.

2. The MMPI is an example of a(n)
   a. projective test.
   b. personality inventory.
   c. intelligence test.
   d. structured clinical interview.

3. The projective hypothesis assumes which of the following?
   a. Responses to highly structured tasks reveal hidden attitudes and motivations.
   b. Preferences for unstructured stimuli reveal unconscious motives.
   c. Unstructured stimuli provoke anxiety.
   d. Responses to ambiguous stimuli are influenced by unconscious factors.

4. The construct validity of intelligence tests is limited by
   a. the way psychologists define intelligence.
   b. the nature of the population tested with the instruments.
   c. their generally low reliability.
   d. none of the above.

5. Which of the following is least likely to be used in behavioural assessment?
   a. projective tests
   b. clinical interviews
   c. self-report inventories
   d. physiological measures

6. When Liz is in the supermarket, she feels increasing anxiety, and she then says to herself, "I just can't stand feeling this feeling." Her self-statement would be the

    a. S.
    b. O.
    c. R.
    d. C.

7. At the heart of Persons and Davidson's model is the mini-theory of the case, or the

    a. diagnostic paradigm.
    b. working hypothesis.
    c. general theory.
    d. problem hypothesis.

8. Which of the following is not one of the variables measured in the McMaster Family Assessment Device?

    a. problem solving
    b. roles
    c. affective responsiveness
    d. intelligence

*9. A brain scan revealed that a man had higher than normal levels of activity in his limbic system. This man probably was having difficulty with

    a. physical movement of the body.
    b. regulation of sleep and arousal.
    c. regulation of emotion.
    d. language formation.

10. Functional MRI (fMRI) differs from ordinary MRI in that

    a. fMRI can record metabolic changes in the brain.
    b. ordinary MRI can only be done annually.
    c. fMRI relies upon other tests to assess brain function.
    d. ordinary MRI is invasive.

*11. Two people the same age, Sarah and Linda, were administered the Luria-Nebraska neuropsychological test battery. Sarah graduated with a Ph.D., while Linda did not complete high school. Assuming all other factors equal, the scores they receive on the Luria-Nebraska

    a. should differ: Sarah should score higher based on education.
    b. should differ: Linda should score higher as it is not based on education.
    c. should not differ since the test controls for education level.
    d. It is impossible to predict the differences.

12. Cultural diversity should lead clinicians to

    a. avoid using most tests with individuals from other cultures.
    b. adhere strictly to DSM criteria in making diagnoses.
    c. be especially alert for pathological behaviour that is acceptable in another culture.
    d. seek information on various cultural practices and views.

13.   The Inuit Norming Study found that

    a.   75% of Inuit children would be classified as "retarded" on the basis of their verbal IQ scores alone.

    b.   using the Wechsler Verbal norms would result in the misclassification of great numbers of Inuit children.

    c.   Inuit children scored within normal ranges on the performance scales of the WISC.

    d.   all of the above.

    e.   none of the above.

SHORT ANSWER

1.   How are reliability and validity related?

2.   Identify one similarity and one difference between normal conversation and clinical interviews.

3.   What types of items are used in lie scales of personality inventories, such as the MMPI?

4.   How have projective tests become more objective over the years?

5.   What are intelligence tests designed to measure or predict?

6.   Dr. Jones is a behavioural psychologist helping the Smiths, who are having "discipline problems" with their child. Dr. Jones would like to directly observe this behaviour without having to spend several days in the Smiths' home waiting for it to occur. What can Dr. Jones do?

7.   Describe the perspective that informs the contemporary view of the role of the family in psychopathology.

8.   What is an advantage of neuropsychological assessment over other biological assessment procedures, such as brain imaging?

9. Canada has many eminent researchers in the field of biological psychology. What subfield does much of the current research focus on?

10. Why can oversensitivity to cultural issues among clinicians be a problem?

ANSWERS TO SELF-TEST, CHAPTER 4

MULTIPLE CHOICE

1. b (p. 100)	2. b (p. 104)	3. d (p. 106)	4. a (p. 108)
5. a (p. 109)	6. b (p. 109)	7. b (p. 109)	8. d (p. 118)
9. c (p. 118)	10. a (p. 118)	11. c (p. 121)	12. d (p. 125)
13. d (p. 126)			

SHORT ANSWER

1. Reliability limits validity. A measure that is not reliable (repeatable) cannot easily be valid (accurate or correct). (p. 100)

2. They are similar in that both are ways of finding out about others. They are different in that interviews only seek information about one person, the interviewee, and pay attention to how the interviewee says things. (p. 101)

3. Lie scales use items that people might like to endorse but cannot do honestly. (p. 104)

4   More objective, standardized scoring methods have been developed. (p. 106)

5. They predict who will succeed in school. (p. 108)

6. Have the Smiths interact with their child in the consulting room while Dr. Jones observes. (p. 115)

7. The family systems perspective is based on the premise that behaviours produced in the family environment reflect the various components that are present in the current family setting. (p. 115)

8. It can detect more subtle changes by looking at how the brain functions rather than changes in its structure. (p. 120)

9. Much Canadian research has focused on neuropsychological assessment, such as the Halstead-Reitan battery for children with learning disabilities. (p. 121)

10. Oversensitivity may lead clinicians to minimize the seriousness of problems by attributing them to subcultural norms. (p. 125)

Chapter 5 Research Methods in the Study of Abnormal Behaviour

OVERVIEW

Earlier chapters have covered paradigms or theories in psychopathology (Chapters 1 and 2) and classification and assessment issues (Chapters 3 and 4). Chapter 5 discusses scientific methods and research designs in abnormal psychology.

Many research issues have already been mentioned in Chapters 1 through 4. At times, it may have seemed as if scientific research creates more confusion than answers. Research can be complex, at least in part because scientists are very concerned about the limitations of their approach and their methods. It is said that there is no perfect research design: each has both strengths and limitations. Chapter 5 describes these strengths and limitations as a basis for understanding research into the various problem behaviours discussed later in the text.

Chapter 5 is the last introductory chapter. Chapter 6 is the first of eleven chapters, comprising parts two and three of the text, discussing the various specific forms of abnormality. Chapters 6 and 7 cover problems related directly or indirectly to anxiety. These disorders used to be referred to as *neuroses*.

CHAPTER SUMMARY

Chapter 5 discusses the methods scientists use to develop systematic knowledge as a basis for evaluating theories and principles.

Science and Scientific Methods discusses basic principles of science. Statements and ideas must be publicly testable and capable of being proven false. Observations must be reliable or repeatable. Theories are propositions that both result from research and generate testable ideas for further research.

The Research Methods of Abnormal Psychology include case studies, epidemiological research, correlational studies, experiments, and single-subject and mixed designs. Each method has advantages and disadvantages. They vary in the kinds of data they produce and the kinds of inferences, especially about causation, that can be drawn from them.

A case study is an extensive description of a particular, often unusual, problem or procedure. It is difficult to develop general principles from them, but they can provide examples to disconfirm principles and generate ideas for further research.

Epidemiological research studies how an illness or characteristic is distributed across the population. Such studies can be helpful in planning treatment needs as well as suggesting possible causes for a problem. As an example of epidemiological research, the role of abuse in the etiology of mental disorders in Canada is explored.

Correlational methods measure the relationship between two (or more) variables (for example, between course grades and anxiety). They are widely used in abnormal psychology, but because they do not actually manipulate variables, it is difficult to draw conclusions about causation from them.

In experiments, researchers manipulate one (or more) independent variables and study the effects of the change on dependent variable(s). Experiments are the preferred method for studying causation. However, in abnormal psychology, many variables cannot be manipulated for practical or ethical reasons. Experiments seek internal validity by using procedures such as control groups and random assignment. External validity is difficult with any research design.

The single-subject ABAB design studies the effect on a single individual's behaviour of repeatedly (a) holding back and (b) applying some manipulation. This design can produce dramatic effects, although generalizability is difficult.

Mixed designs combine correlational and experimental techniques by actively manipulating only some variables.

ESSENTIAL CONCEPTS

1.   Science is the pursuit of systematized knowledge through observation, although it is not purely objective and is influenced by the paradigms of the researcher and of society. Science demands replication of findings and peer-reviewed journals attempt minimize subjectivity.

2.   In order to be considered scientific, ideas must be publicly testable and reliable (or repeatable).

3.   Scientific theories both account for data and generate hypotheses. Theoretical concepts bridge spatial and temporal relations and summarize observed relations.

4.   Case studies lack control and objectivity, but they can be useful for (a) describing unusual phenomena, (b) disconfirming supposedly universal aspects of a theory, and (c) generating hypotheses to be tested through experimentation.

5.   Epidemiological research investigates the frequency and distribution of some problem or variable in the population. Such research is useful for social planning and can suggest causes of a problem.

6.   Correlational methods study the degree of association between two or more variables (for example, IQ and grades). The variables are only observed, not manipulated. Thus, directionality and third-variable problems are difficult to answer, and causal inferences are risky.

7.   Statistical significance refers to a convention adopted by scientists wherein a finding is not considered to be meaningful unless the odds are less than 5 in 100 that it occurred by chance.

8.   An experiment differs from a correlational method because in an experiment one of the variables is actively manipulated and extraneous variables are controlled. When properly conducted, an experiment is a powerful tool for studying causality, but ethical and practical problems often limit its use in studying psychopathology.

9. The basic features of an experiment include the experimental hypothesis, independent variables, dependent variables, and experimental effects.

10. Internal validity refers to whether the results obtained can be confidently attributed to the independent variable. Internal validity is aided by control groups and random assignment to eliminate confounds. There is debate over the role of placebo controls in psychological research.

11. External validity concerns generalizability of a particular study. It is difficult to evaluate.

12. Analogue experiments are frequently used to study psychopathology, but their external validity is always of concern.

13. Single-subject research can dramatically demonstrate a phenomenon in one subject, although generalizability is a problem.

14. Meta-analysis is a new statistic method that allows researchers to combine the results of many different studies that have investigated a similar set of variables.

15. Mixed designs study the effect of several variables, some of which are observed (as in correlational methods) and some of which are actually manipulated (as in the experiment).

KEY TERMS

analogue experiment (p. 147)

directionality problem (p. 142)

case study (p. 135)

double-blind procedure (p. 146)

classificatory variables (p. 142)

epidemiology (p. 137)

confounds (p. 145)

experiment (p. 143)

control group (p. 144)

experimental effect (p. 144)

correlation coefficient (p. 141)

experimental hypothesis (p. 143)

correlational method (p. 140)

external validity (p. 146)

dependent variable (p. 143)

high-risk method (p. 142)

hypotheses (p. 133)

incidence (p. 137)

independent variable (p. 143)

internal validity (p. 145)

meta-analysis (p. 150)

mixed design (p. 149)

moderator variable (p. 151)

parental mental disorder (p. 137)

placebo control group (p. 146)

placebo effect (p. 145)

prevalence (p. 137)

random assignment (p. 143)

reversal (ABAB) design (p. 148)

risk factors (p. 137)

science (p. 133)

severe abuse (p. 137)

single-subject experimental design (p. 147)

statistical significance (p. 141)

theory (p. 133)

third-variable problem (p. 142)

STUDY QUESTIONS

SCIENCE AND SCIENTIFIC METHODS (p. 133)

1. Describe two basic requirements of any scientific approach. Identify two roles of theory. Give two advantages of theoretically inferred concepts in theory design. Give two views on judging the legitimacy of theoretical concepts. (p. 133)

THE RESEARCH METHODS OF ABNORMAL PSYCHOLOGY (p. 134)

2.   List six research methods of abnormal psychology (pp. 134–150). What is a case study (the first method)? Describe three ways in which case studies are useful. What dangers are inherent in the use of this methodology? (p. 134)

3.   What is epidemiology? Describe two uses of epidemiological research in psychopathology. (p. 137)

4.   What are the strongest risk factors identified in the Ontario *Mental Health Supplement* study? (p. 137)

5.   What are correlational methods, and how are they different from experimental research? How are correlations measured and their significance evaluated? (p. 140)

6.   Why are correlational methods often used in studying psychopathology? What is their major drawback and two reasons for it? (p. 140)

7.   How does the experiment overcome the drawback of correlational methods? Identify five basic features of the experimental design. How is the significance of an experimental effect determined? (p. 142)

8.   What is internal validity? Describe how control groups and random assignment are used to eliminate confounds and provide internal validity. (p. 144)

9.   In psychotherapy research, how are placebo effects viewed and controlled? Describe issues in using

placebo controls in psychotherapy research. What is external validity, and why is it difficult to demonstrate? (p. 145)

10. What are analogue experiments? What is an advantage and a disadvantage of using analogues in experimental designs? (p. 146)

11. What is the single-subject ABAB design, and how does it show that the manipulation produced the result? What is the primary disadvantage of this design? (p. 148)

12. What is meta-analysis? Give an example of its use. (p. 150)

13. What is a mixed design? Give examples, explaining why they are mixed designs. Identify an advantage and a disadvantage of mixed designs. (p. 152)

SELF-TEST, CHAPTER 5

(* Items not covered in Study Questions.)

MULTIPLE CHOICE

1. Frequently, theories are developed by
   a. sudden insight.
   b. determining the most useful way to look at a set of data.
   c. pondering the implications of a paradigm.
   d. all of the above.

2. Dr. Roberts noted that whenever her student, Ted, was praised for reading he read more. She then stated that reinforcement increases his behaviour. Using this framework, _____ is a theoretical concept, whereas _____ was derived from the theory to illustrate the concept.

a.   reading; praise
b.   reinforcement; praise
c.   reading; behaviour
d.   reinforcement; reinforcement

3.   Dr. Lee has been treating someone with an unusual combination of symptoms. He notes that there are no published studies on such a combination of symptoms and considers developing a case study. How would Dr. Lee conduct this study?
a.   Try to find other cases like the one he is treating.
b.   Gather detailed historical and biographical information on this single individual.
c.   Examine treatment response using an ABAB design. ✗ single study
d.   Withhold treatment in an effort to fully understand the significance of symptoms.

4.   Epidemiology is the study of
a.   unique cases or unusual disorders. ✗
b.   the rates and correlates of disorders in a population.
c.   the development of disorders over the lifespan. ✗
d.   mental disorders in other cultures.

5.   The strongest risk factors for future mental illness identified in Ontario's mental health study include
a.   early hallucinations or delusions.
b.   parental mental disorder.
c.   severe abuse.
d.   a and c.
e.   none of the above.

6.   Correlational research differs from experimental research in that correlational research
a.   is associated with external validity.
b.   does not involve manipulation of variables.
c.   relies on significance tests.
d.   samples large groups of participants.

7.   Statistical significance in research suggests the results are
a.   internally valid.
b.   externally valid.
c.   not affected by experimenter bias.
d.   not due to chance.

8.   Psychopathologists rely upon correlational research because
a.   it is effective in determining cause and effect. ✗
b.   many of the variables they wish to study cannot be manipulated.
c.   ethical considerations prevent them from doing case studies. ✗
d.   they do not have access to large samples of disordered individuals.

9. Dr. Wilhelm randomly assigned 50 depressed patients (equal numbers of men and women) to two groups for treatment. One group received medication, and the other received cognitive therapy. Ratings of the depression level of the subjects were taken before and after treatment. The rating of subjects' depression level is the

    a.   dependent variable.

    b.   confound variable.

    c.   third variable.

    d.   independent variable.

10. Mary, who has trichotillomania (chronic hair pulling), is using an ABAB design to see if she pulls more hair while watching TV. She watched TV during dinner for four weeks and pulled at least ten hairs a day for the four weeks. Then she left the TV off for four weeks and pulled only one hair per day for the four weeks. In the next step of this design, Mary should

    a.   get other subjects to follow the same procedure.

    b.   have her mother rate how much she eats.

    c.   turn the TV back on for four weeks.

    d.   change what she eats during dinner.

11. Meta-analysis

    a.   combines the results of different statistical methods used on one set of data.

    b.   combines the results of several different studies that looked at similar variables.

    c.   can be used to look for cheating in research studies.

    d.   is no longer used in research.

12. Mixed designs are most useful in

    a.   determining cause and effect.

    b.   identifying which particular treatment is best for which group of patients.

    c.   examining relations between disorders and prevalence.

    d.   obtaining internally valid results.

SHORT ANSWER

1. Young Sigmund Freud was amazed at the number of his clients who reported being sexually abused as children. He could not believe sexual abuse was that common, so he developed the oedipal conflict. This is an example of theory building by using _____ in order to _____.

2. Explain how case studies can be used to disprove general theories.

3. What kind of research design would be used to identify reasons why college students drop out of school?

4. Describe the overall relationship between abuse as a child and the incidence of mental disorders discovered in the Ontario *Mental Health Supplement* study.

5. Explain the "directionality problem" in correlational research.

6. Experiments are said to be internally valid if…

7. Professor Diaz finds that females get better scores than males on his essay tests. He would like to prove that this happens because they give better answers and not because of sexual bias on his part. Describe a double-blind procedure he could use to do this.

8. Why is it difficult to demonstrate external validity?

9. What factors determine whether a research study is an analogue study?

10. In a single-subject ABAB design, how can we be sure that the manipulation produced the result?

11. Give an example of a mixed research design.

12. Discuss an example of the use of meta-analysis.

ANSWERS TO SELF-TEST, CHAPTER 5

MULTIPLE CHOICE

1. a (p. 133)	2. b (p. 134)	3. b (p. 134)	4. b (p. 137)
5. d (p. 137)	6. b (p. 140)	7. d (p. 141)	8. b (p.141)
9. a (p. 143)	10. c (p. 148)	11. b (p. 150)	12. b (p. 149)

SHORT ANSWER

1. (using) an inferred theoretical concept (in order to) bridge spatiotemporal relations. (p. 133)

2. Case studies can provide clear examples that don't work as the theory predicts. (p. 136)

3. Epidemiological research. (p. 137)

4. The Ontario study discovered a correlation between abuse and the likelihood of developing a mental disorder. In the study, 38 percent of people with two or more disorders reported experiencing severe sexual or physical abuse as a child; 21 percent of those with one disorder and 10 percent of healthy individuals reported the same experience. (p. 137)

5. Correlations show that two variables are related but do not show which variable leads to the other. For example, IQ and school grades correlate, which could mean that smart people get better grades or that people who are taught more in school become smarter. (p. 142)

6. The effect can be confidently attributed to manipulating the independent variable. The data from a control group provide a standard against which the effects of an independent variable can be compared. (p. 144)

7. Professor Diaz could have someone else, who would not be involved in grading the tests, remove all names and identifying information from the test papers before he scores them. (p. 146)

8. There is no way to know for sure to what situations results will generalize. The best one can do is perform similar experiments in new situations. (p. 146)

9. The way the results are used determines if it is an analogue study, including what implications are made and what other situations the results are applied to. (p. 146)

10. We can be sure by reversing (introducing and removing) the independent variable repeatedly. When the behaviour repeatedly changes along with the independent variable, we can feel confident that the manipulation produced the change. (p. 148)

11. Your example should include two independent variables, one of which is simply measured (a classificatory variable) and one of which is manipulated. For example, compare test scores of male and female students (a classificatory variable) after they spend two hours hearing a lecture or reading the text (a manipulation). (p. 149)

12. In their original study, Smith et al. (1980) meta-analyzed 475 psychotherapy outcome studies involving more than 25,000 patients and 1,700 effect sizes and came to two conclusions: (a) patients who received treatment were better off than patients who received no treatment and (b) all therapies worked equally well. (p. 150)

Chapter 6 Anxiety Disorders

OVERVIEW

The first five chapters have discussed several basic ideas and issues in abnormal psychology. These concepts provide a framework for surveying the various forms of abnormality. You will want to refer back to these chapters periodically as you study the rest of the text.

The next eleven chapters survey the various forms of abnormality. Now would be a good time to glance over all these chapters. Notice that they cover a wide range of problem behaviours. Several of them are matters of current social debate. The last two chapters in the text discuss issues in intervention as well as legal and ethical issues.

The first two chapters on forms of abnormality, Chapters 6 and 7, discuss problems related directly or indirectly to anxiety. Chapter 6 covers anxiety disorders, which more or less directly involve excessive fears, worries, and anxiety. Chapter 7 discusses two groups of problems where anxiety may be more subtly involved. They are somatoform disorders, characterized by physical symptoms or complaints, and dissociative disorders, involving disturbances in memory and awareness. Although the traditional psychoanalytic term "neurosis" is no longer used to describe these problems, anxiety is still seen as involved in various ways.

Chapters 8 and 9 look at other problems that also involve anxiety but where physical and medical issues are more prominent. Chapter 8 discusses stress effects on general health as well as on psychophysiological disorders such as ulcers and heart conditions, which have long been recognized as involving anxiety and stress. Chapter 9 focuses on eating disorders such as anorexia nervosa, which involve health problems resulting from cultural and other stresses.

CHAPTER SUMMARY

Chapter 6 begins the survey of psychological problems by discussing anxiety disorders. Five kinds of anxiety disorders are discussed.

Phobias are relatively common disorders involving intense, unreasonable, disruptive fears of particular situations. They include (a) specific phobias such as fear of snakes and (b) social phobias such as fear of public embarrassment. Psychoanalysts view phobias as defences against repressed conflicts. Behaviourists have offered models based on avoidance, modelling, and prepared learning to explain phobias. These models, as well as cognitive and biological approaches, have led to treatment approaches.

Panic Disorder involves sudden, unexpected attacks of anxiety. Panic attacks may lead to agoraphobia or fear of leaving safe places. Research suggests that these people escalate stressors into full-blown panic due to their fear-of-fear or fear of loss of control. A focus section reviews research on the prevalence of panic attacks and panic disorders in Canadian university students. People with *Generalized Anxiety Disorder* live in relatively constant tension. People with *Obsessive-Compulsive Disorders* are bothered by unwanted thoughts (obsessions) and/or feel compelled to engage in repetitive rituals (compulsions) to avoid becoming anxious. There are a variety of psychoanalytic, behavioural, cognitive, and biological views on the cause of each disorder that have led to corresponding treatments.

Post-traumatic Stress Disorder (PTSD) reflects the effects of traumatic events such as disasters or combat, which may affect anyone. After-effects include re-experiencing the traumatic event, avoiding stimuli associated with the event, and increased arousal. Treatments emphasize rapid intervention and talking through or reliving the event in a supportive atmosphere. Research at St. Joseph's Hospital in Hamilton, Ontario, on the treatment of anxiety disorders and work on PTSD in Canadian war veterans and peacekeeping troops is discussed.

ESSENTIAL CONCEPTS

1.   Anxiety disorders are believed to have different causes according to different schools of thought. Each school also prescribes different treatments based on their model of the cause.

2.   The major categories of anxiety disorders listed in *DSM-IV* are phobias, panic disorder, generalized anxiety disorder, obsessive-compulsive disorder, and post-traumatic stress disorder.

3.   A phobia is a disrupting, fear-mediated avoidance, out of proportion to the actual danger from the object or situation that is feared.

4.   Psychoanalytic, behavioural, cognitive, and biological models of phobias have been proposed. None account for all phobias. A diathesis model allows for consideration of multiple factors to account more fully for phobias.

5.   Therapies for phobias all emphasize re-experiencing the feared situation. Drugs have also been used but are typically effective only as long as the person continues to take them.

6.   Panic disorders, involving unexpected attacks of anxiety, may lead to agoraphobia or fear of public places. Several biological and psychological approaches are available.

7.   Generalized anxiety disorder, characterized by chronic anxiety, has often been viewed and treated in ways similar to phobias. Treatment approaches seek to help people manage their fears in various ways.

8.   Obsessive-compulsive disorder involves obsessive thoughts and compulsive behaviours. A wide range of causes and treatments have been proposed, with limited success.

9.   Post-traumatic stress disorder (PTSD) is primarily an after-effect of experiencing trauma, although other factors increase the risk of PTSD after a trauma. Canadian research has suggested that the severity of the trauma can be a significant variable and that reactions to traumatic events can last for 50 years.

10.   PTSD is treated in various ways. Typically, treatment stresses immediate intervention, exposure under supportive conditions, and social support.

KEY TERMS

acute stress disorder (p. 180)

agoraphobia (p. 165)

anxiety (p. 155)

anxiety disorders (p. 155)

anxiety sensitivity (p. 169)

anxiolytics (p. 164)

autonomic lability (p. 161)

compulsion (p. 174)

depersonalization (p. 164)

derealization (p. 164)

flooding (p. 163)

generalized anxiety disorder (GAD) (p. 171)

homework (p. 164)

in vivo exposure (p. 162)

obsessions (p. 174)

obsessive-compulsive disorder (OCD) (p. 174)

panic disorder (p. 164)

phobia (p. 156)

post-traumatic stress disorder (PTSD) (p. 180)

social phobias (p. 158)

specific phobias (p. 157)

vicarious learning (p. 159)

virtual reality (VR) exposure (p. 162)

STUDY QUESTIONS

1. Identify two reasons for comorbidity in anxiety disorders. (p. 155)

PHOBIA (p. 156)

2. Summarize three behavioural theories of phobias. Describe recent findings that link social phobia and school drop out. (p. 159)

3. What is the general limitation of behavioural theories, and why would it be helpful to add the idea of "diatheses" to them? Describe four possible diatheses for phobias (social skills, cognitive, autonomic, genetic). (p. 160)

4. Summarize the (a) psychoanalytic, (b) behavioural (five techniques), and (c) cognitive approaches to therapy for phobias. What do all these techniques have in common? What is the key problem with the common biological treatment? (p. 161)

PANIC DISORDER (p. 164)

5. Describe the characteristics of panic disorder and its relation to agoraphobia. Summarize the overall findings with regard to the incidence of panic symptoms in Canadian university studies. How comparable are clinical and subclinical forms of panic? Evaluate four biological and two psychological factors or hypotheses about panic disorder. (p. 165)

6. Identify three disadvantages to biological treatments for panic disorders. Describe two general psychological treatments and compare their effectiveness to biological treatments. (p. 170)

GENERALIZED ANXIETY DISORDER (p. 171)

7.   Describe the characteristics of generalized anxiety disorder. Summarize a psychoanalytic, four cognitive-behavioural, and two biological views on its cause. (p. 172)

8.   Summarize four cognitive-behavioural components in treatment of GAD. Compare the effectiveness of these approaches to drug therapies. Identify the advantages and disadvantages of drug therapies. (p. 173)

OBSESSIVE-COMPULSIVE DISORDER (p. 174)

9.   Define and give several examples of obsessions and of compulsions. How are these definitions different from the way we commonly use the terms? Summarize views on the causes of obsessive-compulsive disorders (two psychoanalytic, three behavioural and cognitive, and three biological views). (p. 174)

10. Briefly summarize five treatments for obsessive-compulsive disorders (including two biological treatments). How effective are treatments for OCD generally? Summarize the treatment procedures used in the case of CC at the Anxiety Treatment and Research Centre, St. Joseph's Healthcare in Hamilton, Ontario. (p. 178)

POST-TRAUMATIC STRESS DISORDER (p. 180)

11. How is post-traumatic stress disorder (PTSD) defined differently from most disorders? Describe three main characteristics of PTSD. Describe risk factors for PTSD, including severity of trauma, dissociative symptoms, and coping style. Describe three theories about its cause. What does Canadian research suggest about variables that contribute to the severity of PTSD symptoms and the length of time that symptoms can persist? (p. 182)

12. Identify two basic principles in treating PTSD. Describe two early approaches to treating veterans with PTSD and the current general approach. Describe three variations on this idea and the use of drugs. (p. 185)

SELF-TEST, CHAPTER 6

(* Items not covered in Study Questions.)

MULTIPLE CHOICE

1. Which of the following is a reason for comorbidity among anxiety disorders?
    a. Anxiety disorder sufferers are often so impaired that they develop additional syndromes.
    b. Many symptoms of anxiety disorders are not exclusively specific to that disorder.
    c. Anxiety is part of almost all psychopathology.
    d. Anxiety is part of a continuum of a variety of disorders.

2. Margaret and Ed have different fears. Margaret is afraid of snakes, whereas Ed is afraid of dogs. Their fears are similar in that
    a. both likely have a similar function.
    b. both require aversive learning consequences for their development.
    c. neither respond well to treatment.
    d. all of the above.

3. Jim was bitten by a goose when he was a child. Now, as an adult, when he goes to ponds where geese flock, he experiences fear and leaves. His anxiety subsides once he leaves. This illustrates the _____ theory of phobias.
    a. two-factor
    b. psychoanalytic
    c. learning
    d. cognitive

4. After viewing tapes of monkeys apparently showing fear of snakes, lambs, and flowers, monkeys who viewed these tapes were fearful only of snakes. This provides only partial support for _____ but better support for _____.
    a. modelling; classical conditioning
    b. vicarious learning; avoidance learning
    c. modelling; preparedness
    d. preparedness; diathesis

5. Cognitive therapy for the treatment of specific phobias is limited by the fact that
    a. some patients have difficulty becoming deeply relaxed.
    b. phobics often become too frightened to discuss their fears directly.
    c. many fears are based on real experiences and thus are not in fact irrational.
    d. phobics already recognize that their fears are unreasonable.

6. Recent findings from Canadian samples suggest that
    a. 10 percent of participants had experienced public speaking anxiety enough to cause them distress.
    b. diagnosed social phobia is associated with marked dissatisfaction in terms of quality of life.
    c. a correlation exists between social phobia and school drop out.

d. all of the above.

e. none of the above.

7. A problem in research that involves creating panics in the lab by hyperventilation has been

    a. convincing panickers to hyperventilate when they are not experiencing a panic.

    b. the low rate of hyperventilation during naturally occurring panics.

    c. an inability to create panics even after long durations of hyperventilation.

    d. inexact amounts of carbon dioxide inhalation.

8. Canadian psychiatrist Jacques Bradwejn has suggested that cholecystokinin (CCK)

    a. is an effective treatment for anxiety disorders.

    b. can induce anxiety-like symptoms in rats.

    c. levels are reduced in individuals with anxiety disorder.

    d. a and c.

    e. none of the above.

9. What diagnosis is most appropriate for Nicole? She is constantly concerned with symmetry, often spending hours arranging items in her room so that the room appears even on the left and right. She also feels that when she eats, the items on the plate must be arranged symmetrically. All of this effort interferes with her work.

    a. obsessive-compulsive disorder

    b. obsessive-compulsive personality disorder

    c. generalized anxiety disorder

    d. specific phobia

10. In the case of CC, two of the most important treatment methods seemed to be

    a. positive reinforcement and negative reinforcement.

    b. free association and interpretation.

    c. changes in diet and small prescriptions for SSRIs.

    d. cognitive restructuring and practice exposure to feared symptoms.

*11. The controversy surrounding post-traumatic stress disorder (PTSD) has been that

    a. most people recover from PTSD within one month.

    b. most people do not develop PTSD after experiencing trauma.

    c. the definition of a traumatic event is so broad as to include almost any stressful human experience.

    d. all of the above.

12. Canadian studies of PTSD suggest that

    a. while trauma from events can be significant, it rarely lasts longer than a year.

    b. while trauma from events can last for many years, it is rarely very significant.

    c. trauma from events can be significant and can last for a very long time.

    d. none of the above.

13. Current psychological treatments for PTSD all emphasize

    a. talking out feelings about the event in a supportive group.

    b. reassurance and rest until memories become less painful.

    c. encouragement to resume normal functioning.

    d. exposure to the traumatic event.

SHORT ANSWER

1.   What assumption was the basis for Freudian models of the cause of anxiety disorders?

2.   Define "social phobia," distinguishing it from specific phobias.

3.   What basis does cognitive research suggest for phobias?

4.   Describe what is done in systematic desensitization as a treatment for phobias.

5.   Describe the overall pattern of findings on panic attacks and panic disorder in Canadian university students.

6.   In what way are panic disorder and generalized anxiety disorder similar?

7.   According to the psychoanalytic view, what is the basis for generalized anxiety?

8.   Mary is chronically anxious. She is very shy and awkward around others. She reports feeling that she can't do anything right. What would a behavioural therapist do to help Mary?

9.   What is the distinction between obsessions and compulsions?

10.   How is PTSD defined differently from most disorders?

11.   Describe the findings of studies done on Canadian veterans with regard to the variables that make the symptoms of PTSD worse and the length of time that symptoms can persist after the event.

ANSWERS TO SELF-TEST, CHAPTER 6

MULTIPLE CHOICE

1. b (p. 155)	2. a (p. 156)	3. a (p.159)	4. c (p. 159)
5. d (p. 163)	6. d (p. 166)	7. b (p. 167)	8. b (p. 167)
9. a (p. 174)	10. d (p. 181)	11. b (p. 182)	12. c (p. 184)
13. d (p. 187)			

SHORT ANSWER

1. Freudians assumed that many problems were based, directly or indirectly, on repressed anxiety. (p. 158)

2. Social phobia is unreasonable fear tied to presence of others or public situations, etc. Specific phobias involve specific situations. Social phobia involves a wide range of situations. (p. 158)

3. Phobic individuals attend to negative events and believe they will reoccur. They focus on future fear-inducing possibilities. (p. 160)

4. The individual is taught how to relax deeply. Then, while relaxed, the person experiences (perhaps, by imagining them) a series of gradually more fearful situations. (p. 162)

5. Overall, this research indicates that panic is a common occurrence among students. Rates for symptoms of panic in one study were as high as 34 percent. A comparison of clinical and subclinical forms of panic found common symptoms for both groups (for example, difficulty concentrating), which suggests a continuity between clinical and nonclinical groups. (p. 166)

6. In generalized anxiety disorder, a person experiences anxiety which is not linked to a particular situation. A panic attack is generally much more specific, with a much more rapid onset and a more intense effect. (p. 166)

7. Generalized anxiety results from conflicts and impulses that have been repressed. The individual is afraid but does not know what he or she is afraid of because it is repressed. Thus, the fear is chronic. (p. 172)

8. Behaviourists would see her anxiety as tied to social fears (a social phobia or cued fear). Relaxation, assertiveness, and social skills training may be appropriate. (p. 173)

9. Obsessions are thoughts, and compulsions are behaviours. (p. 174)

10. The cause or etiology is part of the definition. (p. 182)

11. Canadian studies suggest that the worse the event, the worse the symptoms. POWs who experienced torture had more severe symptoms than other soldiers. Symptoms can persist for at least 50 years, perhaps longer. (p. 184)

Chapter 7 Somatoform and Dissociative Disorders

OVERVIEW

Chapter 7 is the second chapter on disorders related to anxiety and stress. The previous chapter discussed disorders involving fairly direct expressions of anxiety. These included chronic anxiety, phobias or unreasonable fears, and obsessions and compulsions, in which people think and do things in order to control anxiety. Chapter 7 describes disorders in which people may not directly complain of anxiety but have other problems that appear related to anxiety and stress in some way. These are somatoform disorders (involving physical complaints) and dissociative disorders (involving altered memory and awareness). Both arise from psychological factors such as anxiety and stress.

Chapters 8 and 9 then discuss how anxiety and stress can lead to illness and physical or tissue changes. Traditionally, we have recognized the role of stress in psychophysiological disorders such as ulcers. However, we now recognize that stress can play a role in virtually all physical/medical problems. Chapter 8 discusses both these roles. Chapter 9 discusses eating disorders such as anorexia nervosa, which also involve anxiety and physical problems. However, eating disorders also involve significant social and cultural issues.

CHAPTER SUMMARY

Chapter 7 covers two groups of disorders in which there is a loss of functioning with no physical basis. The symptoms seem to serve a psychological purpose. There is considerable controversy about this set of disorders, and many researchers have argued that they should not be included in *DSM-V.*

Somatoform Disorders are characterized by physical complaints that have no physiological basis. The chapter emphasizes two of these disorders. Conversion disorder involves a loss of sensory or motor functioning: for example, a loss of vision, touch, etc., or of the ability to walk, talk, etc. Somatization disorder refers to multiple physical complaints (headaches, various pains, fatigue, etc.) and typically involves repeated visits to physicians for medical treatment.

Knowledge about somatoform disorders is limited, because individuals with these problems typically seek medical, not psychological, treatment. Existing theories deal primarily with conversions. Psychoanalysts propose that repressed conflicts are "converted" into the physical symptoms in various ways and seek to uncover what was repressed. Behavioural theorists suggest that the behaviours reduce anxiety and seek to teach more effective behaviours.

Dissociative Disorders are disorders of awareness and memory. A majority of average people experience some dissociative symptoms in their lifetime. In dissociative amnesia, the individual is unable to recall important personal information, often of traumatic events.

Dissociative fugue involves a more encompassing memory loss, in which the person leaves home and assumes a new identity. Depersonalization disorder is characterized by disconcerting alternations in perception of the self. In dissociative identity disorder (DID), two or more separate and distinct personalities occur in alternation, each having its own memories, behaviours, and life styles. The reality of DID is currently debated in the field.

Psychological theories propose that memory losses in dissociative disorders protect the individual from traumatic memories, perhaps of childhood abuse. Another theory suggests they are learned social roles. Because these disorders strongly suggest repression, psychoanalytic techniques are often used in treatment. In addition to watching for signs of childhood traumatic experiences, clinicians are cautioned to look for signs of false memories of traumatic experiences and to be careful not to induce false memories.

ESSENTIAL CONCEPTS

1. A group of prominent researchers recently presented the radical argument that somatoform disorders should be removed from the pending *DSM-V.* The authors listed several concerns, many of which apply to other diagnostic categories.

2. Conversion disorder and somatization disorder are two major categories of somatoform disorders.

3. In conversion disorders, muscular or sensory functions are impaired with no apparent physical basis so that the symptoms seem to be linked to psychological factors.

4. It is difficult to distinguish between conversion disorder, physical illness, and malingering.

5. Somatization disorder is characterized by recurrent multiple somatic complaints for which medical attention is sought but which have no apparent physical basis.

6. Conversion disorders occupy a historic place in psychoanalytic thinking because their nature led Freud to theorize about the unconscious. Psychoanalysis developed as a technique to overcome these repressed impulses.

7. Behaviourists suggest that conversions are caused by reinforcement, and treatment should focus on teaching more effective ways to get reinforcers.

8. Cognitive psychologists suggest that somatoform and conversion disorders are caused by faulty ideas, assumptions, and thoughts. Cognitive therapy focuses on challenging and eliminating faulty concepts and replacing them with more constructive ones.

9. Dissociative disorders (dissociative amnesia, dissociative fugue, depersonalization, and dissociative identity disorder) involve disruptions of consciousness, memory, and identity. In addition to watching for signs of childhood traumatic experiences, clinicians are cautioned to look for signs of false memories of traumatic experiences and to be careful not to induce false memories.

10. The memory losses in dissociative disorders resemble psychoanalytic concepts of repression. Thus, psychoanalytic techniques are widely used in treating these disorders.

KEY TERMS

anesthesias (p. 196)

body dysmorphic disorder (p. 195)

conversion disorder (p. 196)

depersonalization disorder (p. 207)

dissociative amnesia (p. 205)

dissociative disorders (p. 194)

dissociative fugue (p. 207)

dissociative identity disorder (DID) (p. 208)

factitious disorder (p. 198)

hypochondriasis (p. 195)

hysteria (p. 197)

la belle indifférence (p. 198)

malingering (p. 198)

pain disorder (p. 195)

somatization disorder (p. 199)

somatoform disorders (p. 194)

STUDY QUESTIONS

SOMATOFORM DISORDERS (p. 194)

1. What are the general characteristics of somatoform disorders? Describe and distinguish among three types of somatoform disorders. (These are not discussed in detail.) (p. 194)

2. Give some examples of conversion symptoms involving loss of (a) muscular and (b) sensory functioning. Why is it difficult, but important, to distinguish between conversions and medical conditions? (p. 196)

3. Describe somatization disorder. How is it similar to and different from conversion disorder? List several proposed causes of somatization disorder. (p. 199)

4. How did the study of conversions lead Freud to important concepts? Summarize Freud's early theory of conversions and his later revision of it. (p. 196)

5. Summarize contemporary psychodynamic research on conversions and the resulting revision of Freud's theory. (p. 197)

6. Describe three other approaches to conversion disorders. How well is each supported by research? (p. 197)

7. Why has little research been done on the psychological treatment of somatoform disorders? Summarize current treatment of somatoform disorders in terms of managing (a) anxiety and depression, (b) medical complaints, and (c) giving up symptoms. (p. 202)

DISSOCIATIVE DISORDERS (p. 204)

8. Define and distinguish among four dissociative disorders. Explain how controversy about dissociative identity disorder has been influenced by (a) changes in prevalence, (b) confusion with schizophrenia, and (c) popular cases. Describe Ross's data on the prevalence of dissociative symptoms in the general population of Winnipeg, and consider possible misdiagnosis of these due to cultural differences. (p. 204)

9. Explain the general view of the mechanism underlying dissociative disorders. Describe two major theories of the cause of DID and a study supporting each. (p. 209)

10.   Summarize general principles and goals for treating dissociative disorders in general and dissociative identity disorder in particular. (p. 212)

SELF-TEST, CHAPTER 7

(* Items not covered in Study Questions.)

MULTIPLE -CHOICE

*1.   Somatoform and dissociative disorders are similar in that both
   a.   have symptoms suggesting a physical dysfunction.
   b.   typically begin after a stressful experience.
   c.   involve disruptions of consciousness.
   d.   are delusional in quality.

2.   Jaclyn is preoccupied with her eyes, feeling that they are asymmetrical. She spends hours applying makeup in an effort to make her eyes appear exactly the same size and shape. The extent of her routine has cost her several jobs. She has had plastic surgery, but this has not alleviated her concerns. The most likely diagnosis for Jaclyn would be
   a.   body dysmorphic disorder.
   b.   conversion disorder.
   c.   hypochondriasis.
   d.   somatization disorder.

3.   The onset of conversion symptoms is usually
   a.   sudden and related to a stressful situation.
   b.   gradual and subtle.
   c.   accompanied by great psychological distress.
   d.   preceded by a period of physical illness.

4.   Tony has four major pain symptoms, namely headache, lower back pain, a knee injury, and tinnitus. He complains of ulcers and frequent diarrhea and, although there is no neurological basis, experiences numbness and tingling in his hands. Which of the following additional symptoms would confirm a diagnosis of somatization disorder?
   a.   erectile dysfunction
   b.   preoccupation with a bodily feature
   c.   obsessions
   d.   panic attacks

5.   The performance of a hysterically blind person on a visual test appears to depend on
   a.   their motivation to maintain their symptom.
   b.   the degree of physical impairment.

     c.   the neurological basis for their symptom.

     d.   their unconscious need to please the experimenter.

6.   If the behavioural view of conversion disorder were accurate, what would be true regarding experimental research on visual perception among the hysterically blind?

     a.   They would accurately perceive images shown below conscious awareness.

     b.   They would not be able to accurately respond to images presented to them.

     c.   They would also exhibit other symptoms that would impair other cognitive processes.

     d.   They would begin to show difficulties in other sensory modalities.

*7.   Contemporary researchers focus on _____ anxiety rather than hypochondriasis per se.

     a.   composite

     b.   disease

     c.   health

     d.   free-floating

8.   Among the dissociative disorders, dissociative fugue is characterized by

     a.   massive repression.

     b.   moving away and establishing a new identity.

     c.   sudden development following severe stress.

     d.   memory loss for virtually all past events.

9.   What does Ross conclude from his study of dissociative symptoms in the general population of Winnipeg?

     a.   A majority of people report having at least a few dissociative experiences.

     b.   A minority of people report having at least a few dissociative experiences.

     c.   A small number of people report having no dissociative experiences.

     d.   A small number of people report having any dissociative experiences.

     e.   a and c

     f.   b and c

10.   The categorization of depersonalization as a dissociative disorder is controversial because

     a.   there are no somatic symptoms.

     b.   there is no associated anxiety.

     c.   there is no disturbance in memory.

     d.   there is a heightened sensory awareness.

11.   According to one current theory, dissociative identity disorder develops in people who were _____ as children.

     a.   abused

     b.   overindulged

     c.   unloved

     d.   made to feel guilty

12.   According to Spanos, dissociative identity disorder is
      a.   a very real and painful disorder.
      b.   a uniquely Canadian disorder.
      c.   a form of role playing.
      d.   a physical disorder.

*13. Whereas the DSM is currently a symptom-based method for rendering diagnoses, the classification of dissociative identity disorder shows that diagnosis may be
      a.   based on function.
      b.   dimensional.
      c.   theory driven.
      d.   based upon personality traits.

SHORT ANSWER

1.   Discuss two of the arguments in favour of removing somatoform disorders from the *DSM-V.*

2.   What are the characteristics of hypochondriasis?

3.   Distinguish between conversion disorder and somatization disorder.

4.   How did the study of conversions lead Freud to important concepts?

5.   Describe the psychodynamic studies that led to a contemporary revision of Freud's theory of conversions.

6.   Summarize a behavioural account of the cause of conversion disorders.

7.   What has the research shown about genetic and physiological factors in conversion disorders?

8.   Why has little research been done on the psychological treatment of somatoform disorders?

9.   Describe the cause of the dissociative symptoms of the young Inuit discussed by Seltzer.

10.   Give several reasons why the existence of dissociative identity disorder is disputed.

11.   Discuss the findings and conclusions of the Colin Ross study of dissociative experiences in Winnipeg.

12.   Dissociative disorders (more than other disorders) are commonly treated by psychoanalytic methods because . . .

13.   Discuss the conclusions of Nicholas Spanos about the cause of dissociative identity disorder.

14.   Discuss Prout and Dopson's conclusions about the controversy of repressed memory of childhood sexual abuse vs. the possibility of false memories.

ANSWERS TO SELF-TEST, CHAPTER 7

MULTIPLE CHOICE

1. b (p. 194)	2. a (p. 195)	3. a (p. 196)	4. a (p. 199)
5. a (p. 200)	6. b (p. 201)	7. c (p. 203)	8. b (p. 206)
9. e (p. 208)	10. c (p. 208)	11. a (p. 209)	12. c (p. 210)
13. a (p. 211)			

SHORT ANSWER

1.   The terminology of the somatoform category is often unacceptable to patients. The distinction between symptoms that are disease-based vs. those that are psychogenic may be more apparent than real. (p. 194)

2.   Hypochondriasis is the preoccupation with fear of having a serious medical illness. (p. 195)

3.   Conversion symptoms emphasize a loss of functioning, while somatization disorder symptoms emphasize complaints about loss of functioning. The distinction can be difficult to determine in practice. (p. 194)

4.   Their existence led him to emphasize the unconscious. He argued that if medical causes and deliberate faking are ruled out, then the cause had to be the unconscious. (p. 196)

5.   Case studies in which individuals with conversions involving blindness were able to "guess" visual stimuli much better or worse than could be attributed to chance. (p. 197)

6.   The behaviours are learned. The individual may have learned (through modelling) that sick people behave this way, or their behaviours may be reinforced by attention and getting out of things. (p. 201)

7. These factors are not very important. Genetic twin research has yielded negative results (though right-brain, left-brain research has raised interesting speculations). (p. 202)

8. These people resist the idea that psychological approaches could help what they view as physical problems. Thus they are rarely available for study. (p. 202)

9. Seltzer describes a young Inuit boy treated for dissociative disorder who developed his "symptoms" due, in part, to his cultural beliefs in spirit possession. (p. 206)

10. The rate of DID diagnoses has varied widely, apparently depending on popular writings. DID was an issue in several highly publicized trials. (p. 208)

11. Psychiatrist Colin Ross looked for experiences typical of DID among the general population of Winnipeg. His research indicates that some experiences associated with dissociation are quite common. While dissociative experiences are infrequent and transient in the general population, his research suggests that DID consists of an exaggeration or increase in frequency of normally occurring experiences. (p. 216)

12. Psychoanalytic concepts such as the unconscious and repression clearly seem applicable. (p. 213)

13. Spanos challenges the validity of DID as a distinct psychiatric disorder. His cognitive behavioural model of hypnosis led him to the conclusion that DID is basically role playing encouraged by clinicians who encourage the patient to take on this particular role. (p. 210)

14. Prout and Dobson suggested that the best approach right now is a "middle ground perspective," where it is recognized that child abuse can be quite legitimate, but there is also the possibility that certain clinicians may have facilitated false reports. Each case should be evaluated individually without preconceptions. (p. 213)

Chapter 8 Psychophysiological Disorders and Health Psychology

OVERVIEW

The last two chapters covered psychological disorders linked to anxiety. Chapters 8 and 9 cover problems related to anxiety in more complex ways. The disorders covered in Chapters 6 and 7 have traditionally been referred to as *neuroses*. Those in Chapter 6 involved more or less direct difficulties with anxiety. The disorders described in Chapter 7 do not directly involve anxiety but anxiety is traditionally believed to underlie them. They are somatoform disorders (involving physical symptoms) and dissociative disorders (involving memory, consciousness, and identity). All the problems in Chapter 7 involve physical complaints without physically detectable changes in the body. In contrast, the problems covered in Chapter 8 do involve physically detectable changes.

It should be clear by now that anxiety is a source of much psychological suffering. Anxiety and stress also have physical effects. Some of these, such as heart disease, ulcers, and asthma, have traditionally been termed *psychophysiological disorders*. However, that term has been discarded with the realization that stress is a factor in illness and health generally. Chapter 8 discusses stress and health as well as the psychophysiological disorders.

Chapter 9 covers eating disorders, such as anorexia nervosa. Eating disorders also involve physical problems and tissue change. They surely result from anxiety and stress, broadly defined. However, more specifically, they appear related to cultural pressures to control weight, especially among women.

After Chapter 9, the text shifts focus. Chapters 10 and 11 cover mood disorders (such as depression) and schizophrenia. These are more complex problems, at least in terms of treatment and research (especially physiological research).

CHAPTER SUMMARY

Chapter 8 focuses on the role of psychological factors in physical illnesses generally. Psychological factors have been considered especially strong in medical conditions traditionally referred to as *psychophysiological disorders*. However, DSM has dropped that term, recognizing that psychological factors contribute to some degree to virtually all medical illnesses. The chapter discusses some common examples of psychophysiological disorders in detail.

Stress and Health reviews efforts to define and measure stress and its relation to physical illness in general. *Theories of the Stress-Illness Link* describes several biological and psychological theories regarding this relationship. The contributions of Hans Selye, seen by many as the originator of the empirical study of stress, and Canadian research on the ameliorating effects of humour on stress are also discussed. There is a direct link between the autonomic nervous system and stress. This system is activated during stress and is affected by chronic stress. Efforts to measure stress for research and diagnostic purposes are discussed.

Cardiovascular Disorders, including hypertension and heart disease, appear related to specific styles of responding to stress, especially Type A behaviour and cynicism/anger. *Socio-economic Status, Ethnicity, and Health* discusses socio-economic and ethnic differences in health and longevity. While genetic factors cannot be ruled out, differences are largely related to such factors as access to care, lifestyles, and social stress.

Therapies for Psychophysiological Disorders involve treating current symptoms and underlying conditions using both medical and psychological approaches. Psychological approaches are used to reduce risk factors, to change general psychological contributors, and to teach specific skills. Behavioural medicine, a new specialization, is developing specialized psychological techniques to treat psychophysiological disorders and other medical conditions. The treatment of chronic pain in Canada is an example of the application of the principles of behavioural medicine.

ESSENTIAL CONCEPTS

1. Psychophysiological disorders are distinct from conversion reactions and involve physical tissue changes that are caused or worsened by emotional factors.

2. *DSM-IV* does not list psychophysiological disorders because virtually all physical illnesses are now viewed as potentially related to psychological factors.

3. Stress has been defined in various ways, including stressful events, stress responses, and coping skills.

4. If a person is chronically stressed, this means that the sympathetic nervous system is also chronically activated and, eventually, significant health problems may result from this activation and prolonged exposure to stress hormones.

5. Several research approaches indicate relationships between stress and illness. Coping skills and social supports influence these relationships.

6. There are both biological and psychological theories about the link between stress and illness.

7. There is much research on psychological factors contributing to cardiovascular disorders.

8. High blood pressure and coronary heart disease appear related to Type A behaviours, especially the suppression of anger, although this research is complex and ongoing.

9. Asthma apparently results from a combination of physical and psychological factors whose importance varies with the individual.

10. Health and longevity vary among various socio-economic and ethnic groups. These differences appear, at least largely, to be the result of differing access to services, lifestyles, stresses, and similar factors.

11. Where psychological factors contribute to illness, a combination of medical and psychological treatment is needed.

12. Behavioural medicine is developing specific programs for treating psychological factors that contribute to illness.

KEY TERMS

allostatic load (p. 224)

anger-in theory (p. 233)

angina pectoris (p. 239)

autonomic nervous system (p. 222)

behavioural medicine (p. 221)

biofeedback (p. 243)

cardiovascular disorders (p. 235)

catastrophization (p. 249)

chronic pain (p. 249)

coping (p. 224)

coronary heart disease (CHD) (p. 238)

daily hassles (p. 227)

distress (p. 222)

emotional support (p. 229)

essential hypertension (p. 235)

eustress (p. 222)

functional social support (p. 229)

general adaptation syndrome (GAS) (p. 221)

goodness of fit hypothesis (p. 224)

health psychology (p. 221)

instrumental support (p. 229)

interactionism (p. 228)

job burnout (p. 227)

job spillover (p. 227)

job stress (p. 227)

myocardial infarction (p. 239)

palliative coping (p. 229)

parasympathetic nervous system (p. 222)

psychological factors affecting medical condition (p. 220)

stress (p. 221)

psychophysiological disorders (p. 220)

stress management (p. 247)

psychosomatic disorders (p. 220)

stressor (p. 223)

self-efficacy (p. 223)

structural social support (p. 229)

social gradient of health (p. 241)

sympathetic nervous system (p. 222)

somatic nervous system (p. 222)

Type A behaviour pattern (p. 239)

somatic-weakness theory (p. 231)

vital exhaustion (p. 227)

specific-reaction theory (p. 231)

STUDY QUESTIONS

1. Define psychophysiological disorders, distinguishing them from conversion disorders (in Chapter 7). How does *DSM-IV* handle psychophysiological disorders? How does this approach lead to broader understandings of the relationship between stress and illness? (p. 220)

STRESS AND HEALTH (p. 221)

2. Summarize the general adaptation syndrome (GAS), as introduced by Hans Selye, and explain his distinction between negative and positive forms of stress. (p. 221)

3. Describe three approaches to defining stress and the limitations of each. (p. 221)

4. Describe the relationship between the autonomic nervous system and stress. (p. 222)

5. Describe two efforts to measure stress. The first study uses a retrospective approach. Why is this approach problematic, and how is the second study an improvement? Describe how coping is commonly assessed. (p. 225)

6. Describe two social moderators of stress. How do they influence the relationship between stress and illness? (p. 229)

7. Describe our current understanding of the correlation between humour, stress, and well-being. (p. 227)

THEORIES OF THE STRESS–ILLNESS LINK (p. 230)

8. What kinds of questions are confronted by theories of the stress–illness link? Briefly describe two reasons to be cautious about all these theories. Describe four biological theories and two psychological theories. (p. 230)

CARDIOVASCULAR DISORDERS (p. 235)

9. What is essential hypertension, and how much of a problem is it? Describe the methods and results of (a) two ways of studying the relation between psychological stress and blood pressure increases and (b) two predisposing factors in chronic increases or hypertension. (p. 235)

10. Summarize the Canadian data on the relationship between stress and cardiovascular disease and hypertension. What progress is being made in Canada in hypertension prevention programs? (p. 236)

11. Describe two principal forms of coronary heart disease (CHD). Identify some traditional physical and psychological risk factors for CHD. (p. 238)

12. What limitation of traditional risk factors led to a search for diatheses to CHD? Describe Type A behaviour as a possible psychological diathesis, and identify three psychological factors that have emerged from more recent research. Describe two possible biological diatheses. (p. 239)

SOCIO-ECONOMIC STATUS, ETHNICITY, AND HEALTH (p. 241)

13. Illustrate the role of socio-economic status and ethnicity in health generally. What kinds of psychological factors may underlie these differences? (p. 241)

THERAPIES FOR PSYCHOPHYSIOLOGICAL DISORDERS (p. 242)

14. Why are both medical and psychological interventions needed in treating psychophysiological disorders? Describe more specific programs in five areas: hypertension (methods aimed at risk factors, exercise, relaxation, and cognitions), biofeedback, Type A behaviour, stress management, and pain management (acute and chronic). (p. 242)

15. Describe the cognitive factors and cognitive-based models that have been found to be important in rehabilitation of cardiac patients in Canadian studies. (p. 244)

16. Summarize three methods of stress management present in the text. (p. 247)

SELF-TEST, CHAPTER 8

(* Items not covered in Study Questions.)

MULTIPLE CHOICE

1. Which of the following views was fostered when DSM began requiring diagnostic judgements of psychological factors affecting medical conditions?
    a. Certain physical problems are caused by psychological stress.
    b. Certain psychological problems are caused by physical stress.
    c. All medical problems may result, in part, from psychological factors.
    d. All psychological problems may result, in part, from medical factors.

2. The most effective type of coping has been found to be
    a. inward-focused coping.
    b. problem-focused coping.
    c. emotion-focused coping.
    d. None of the above is always most effective; it depends on the situation.

3. A problem with studies on the link between psychological factors and physical health has been
    a. a general inability of respondents to report physical problems.
    b. over-reporting of physical illness among individuals with high neuroticism.
    c. under-reporting of physical illness among individuals with high psychoticism.
    d. the non-uniform nature of physical illness and associated psychological distress.

4. Lazarus (1966) developed a model of stress based on the premise that stress is not solely due to the situation or to an individual's cognitive appraisals and coping responses; rather, stress results from a transaction or interaction between situational factors and factors inside the person. This is an example of which type of model?
    a. multi-factor
    b. attitudinal
    c. interactional
    d. transactional

*5. Studies often show that not only does a link exist between self-reported daily _____ and poor psychological and physical adjustment, but that they are often better than measures of major _____ at predicting adjustment problems.
    a. events
    b. traumas
    c. hassles
    d. problems

6. Which of the following is not a predisposing factor in hypertension?
    a. social isolation
    b. getting angry easily

c. sensitivity to salt

d. sedentary lifestyle

7. In the Western Collaborative Group Study, after traditional risk factors were controlled for, Type A subjects

a. were twice as likely to develop coronary heart disease (CHD) as other subjects.

b. had only a slightly increased risk for developing CHD.

c. were actually less likely to develop CHD than other subjects.

d. were more likely to develop CHD only if they also had a parental history of heart attacks.

8. Which of the following was not a finding of the study on the prevention and control of hypertension in Canada?

a. A key factor that undermined previous prevention programs was the small amount of money (1–2 percent of health care budgets) set aside for prevention.

b. Saskatchewan had the least effective plan for program follow-up and coordination.

c. Expanded lifestyle counselling was needed.

d. Poverty and low education contribute to increased rates of hypertension.

9. The newly proposed Type D personality

a. is closely associated with emotional expression.

b. has been defined as negative affect in conjunction with inhibition in expression.

c. has been shown to be a protective factor from coronary heart disease.

d. is similar to Type A personality but is less severe.

10. Which of the following is a feature of the "gate-control" theory of pain proposed by Melzack and Wall of McGill University?

a. Nerve impulses connoting pain reach the spinal column and, if sufficiently strong, open a "gate" that allows a pain signal to be sent to the brain.

b. Pain gates at the peripheral nerves control whether or not pain signals are sent to the spinal column.

c. The brain sends signals to the spinal column that affect the pain gate.

d. a and c

e. all of the above

11. Biofeedback is

a. a technique used to train people to control otherwise involuntary physical activity.

b. generally ineffective in treating essential hypertension.

c. useful in focusing attention on the physical problems.

d. equivalent to a placebo.

SHORT ANSWER

1. Psychophysiological disorders are not a category in _DSM-IV_ because . . .

2.   Why was it difficult to apply Selye's theory of stress to psychology?

3.   Summarize the relationship between humour and stress found by several Canadian researchers.

4.   Define "functional social support."

5.   Summarize the somatic-weakness theory.

6.   How does psychoanalysis account for the fact that people develop different psychophysiological disorders when exposed to the (apparently) same stressors?

7.   How important a health problem is essential hypertension?

8.   According to research, blood pressure increases in individuals who respond to chronic stress by doing what?

9.   List the three main cognitive factors that influence health risk found by Irvine and Ritvo.

10.   What is the most important reason for ethnic and racial differences in overall health and longevity?

11.   Describe the treatment for Type A behaviour.

ANSWERS TO SELF-TEST, CHAPTER 8

MULTIPLE CHOICE

1. c (p. 220)	2. d (p. 224)	3. b (p. 240)	4. d (p. 224)
5. c (p. 227)	6. d (p. 231)	7. a (p. 240)	8. b (p. 240)
9. b (p. 241)	10. d (p. 248)	11. a (p. 243)	

SHORT ANSWER

1.   Virtually all physical diseases are recognized as potentially related to psychological stress. (p. 220)

2.   It was not clear how stress should be defined: in terms of stimuli, responses, or individual differences in ability to cope. (p. 221)

3.   Several Canadian studies have linked humour with reduced stress, increased psychological well-being, immune system activity, lower blood pressure for women, and higher blood pressure for men. (p. 227)

4.   Functional social support refers to the quality of an individual's friendships—having close friends that can be called on in time of need. (p. 229)

5.   Disorders will appear in whichever physical system is weakest or most vulnerable to stress. (p. 231)

6.   Unconscious, unresolved conflicts influence how individuals respond to stress, thereby producing different disorders. (p. 233)

7.   Called the "silent killer" (because people aren't aware of and don't check their blood pressure), essential hypertension is the cause of 90 percent of cases of high blood pressure, which in turn contributes to many medical problems. (p. 235)

8.   Holding their anger in; not responding; remaining angry and resentful. (p. 236)

9.   Risk expectancy (appraisals of the likelihood of harm if no risk reduction measures are taken), risk-reduction expectancy (judgements of the efficacy of risk reduction actions), attention regulation (the ability of individuals to focus their attention on specific activities). (p. 236)

10.   The most important reasons are lifestyle and socio-economic differences, such as access to health care. Biological factors are of some importance in some illnesses but less important overall. (p. 241)

11.   Multifaceted programs encouraging more relaxed behaviours (talking more slowly, listening more), reducing anger and stress from TV and work, cognitive changes to stop seeing everything as a challenge that must be met, etc. (p. 244)

Chapter

9 Eating Disorders

OVERVIEW

This is the last of four chapters covering topics related to anxiety and stress. Previous chapters (Chapters 6 and 7) discussed psychological disorders related to anxiety and stress in various ways, while the last one, Chapter 8, discussed effects of anxiety and stress on medical illnesses and on the body generally. We have long recognized stress's contribution to psychophysiological disorders (such as ulcers); however, that term has been dropped with recognition that stress can play a role in virtually all physical problems.

Chapter 9 turns to another set of disorders, eating disorders, that also involve physical effects of anxiety and stress. Eating disorders, such as anorexia nervosa, involve physical changes severe enough to be fatal. They certainly involve anxiety and stress. However, in this case, the anxiety and stress seem to result from cultural pressures on people, especially young women, to control their weight.

After Chapter 9, the text focuses on two disorders that are more complex: mood disorders, such as depression (Chapter 10), and schizophrenia (Chapter 11). Both have been widely studied and, for various reasons, much of the research has focused on genetic and physiological issues.

CHAPTER SUMMARY

Clinical Description of three disorders is provided. Anorexia nervosa involves inadequate food intake so that the victim, usually female, may starve to death. Bulimia, in which individuals gorge themselves and then purge the food by vomiting or using laxatives, is less life-threatening but can also have serious physical consequences. Binge eating disorder (a proposed diagnosis for further study in *DSM-IV*) describes individuals who experience recurrent eating binges without purging or weight loss (indeed, commonly with weight gain or fluctuation). Binge eating disorder is not well understood and is not discussed further.

Etiology of Eating Disorders appears to be complex and variable. Biological factors have been hypothesized based on genetic data and knowledge of brain mechanisms in eating. Socio-cultural factors are strongly suggested by correlations between eating disorders and social pressure to be thin, as reflected in advertising, etc. Other views have focused on childhood, personality, and family or abuse issues. Cognitive-behavioural views emphasize irrational beliefs about the necessity of being thin and about controlling eating in order to be acceptable.

Treatment of Eating Disorders describes problems in treating these complex conditions. Biological treatment using antidepressants has yielded mixed results. Anorexics can be kept alive by hospitalizing them to maintain their weight. Treatment of issues underlying anorexia and bulimia has been more difficult, with various methods to address the potential combination of family, social, and psychological factors. Canadian prevention programs have been inventive in several ways, and several comprehensive treatment and prevention programs exist in Canada.

ESSENTIAL CONCEPTS

1. Two long-recognized eating disorders are anorexia nervosa (in which people do not eat) and bulimia nervosa (in which people have eating binges followed by purging).

2. Binge eating disorder, describing individuals who have eating binges without purging, is proposed in *DSM-IV* as a new diagnosis for further study.

3. It has been suggested that some people become anorexic because of a pursuit of fitness, rather than a pursuit of thinness. They have outlined a theory of a phenomenon that they describe as *activity anorexia.* This concept refers to the loss of appetite when engaged in physical activity.

4. Eating disorders may have a genetic liability, although adoption studies are needed to verify this. Brain chemicals involved in controlling normal appetite may be disrupted in eating-disordered individuals.

5. Psychological causes of eating disorders include cultural standards for thinness, cultural factors, gender issues, parent-child relationships, racial factors, and personality characteristics such as perfectionism and low self-esteem.

6. Dynamic views stress developmental factors, such that extreme thinness becomes a side effect of establishing independence. Family systems views propose that eating problems allow the family to ignore larger conflicts. Recent research has found a correlation between narcissism and perfectionism and eating disorders. Personality and family data are difficult to interpret but lend some support.

7. Cognitive-behavioural views suggest that these individuals have unrealistic beliefs about the necessity of being thin and/or have poor skills in moderating their eating.

8. Antidepressants have shown some success in treating bulimia, although drop-out rates are high.

9. Anorexics may require hospitalization to manage medical complications. Providing social reinforcers for eating and weight gain has been somewhat successful. Treatment focuses on challenging beliefs about being thin, developing self-control, and building normal eating behaviours. Treatment of underlying issues (and long-term weight maintenance) is difficult.

10. Bulimia has been treated with some effectiveness using both cognitive-behavioural and interpersonal psychotherapy. However, only about half of patients show improvements that last over time.

11. Several Canadian programs have attempted to prevent eating disorders through such innovative techniques as having the target audience take an active role in the design of the program and presenting prevention programs in high risk settings, such as ballet schools.

12. St. Paul's Hospital, British Columbia Children's Hospital, and ANAB Quebec offer a variety of treatment and outreach programs for the treatment and prevention of eating disorders.

KEY TERMS

activity anorexia (p. 265)

bulimia nervosa (p. 259)

amenorrhea (p. 256)

false hope syndrome (p. 266)

anorexia nervosa (p. 256)

lateral hypothalamus (p. 262)

binge eating disorder (p. 260)

Scarlett O'Hara effect (p. 263)

STUDY QUESTIONS

CLINICAL DESCRIPTION (p. 256)

1. Three diagnostic labels are identified. For each label, summarize (a) the distinguishing features, (b) the subtypes, (c) the relationship to other psychological problems, (d) the physical effects, and (e) the prognosis. (Note that binge eating disorder is a tentative label and not yet well understood.) (p. 256)

2. Describe Canadian rates of eating disorders. (p. 255)

ETIOLOGY OF EATING DISORDERS (p. 261)

3. Under biological factors, what data suggests a genetic contribution to eating disorders? Describe how three areas of brain research may be related to eating disorders. (p. 262)

4. Briefly describe studies of social influences on eating disorders in four areas (socio-cultural variables in industrialized countries, gender influences, cross-cultural studies, and racial differences). (p. 263)

5. Summarize the basis of eating disorders according to Bruch's psychodynamic view and Minuchin's family systems view. Summarize what has been found about the personalities, the families, and the backgrounds of individuals with eating disorders. (p. 267)

6. Summarize the role of narcissism and perfectionism as possible factors in the etiology of eating disorders. (p. 269)

7. Summarize the cognitive-behavioural view of anorexia nervosa and of bulimia nervosa. (p. 270)

TREATMENT OF EATING DISORDERS (p. 271)

8. Summarize the effectiveness of biological treatment of bulimia (including two problems) and of anorexia. (p. 271)

9. Describe the cognitive-behavioural model of treatment proposed by Fairburn et al., and discuss its emphasis on self-control. (p. 273)

10. Describe the goals, methods, and effectiveness of two stages in treating anorexia. Describe Minuchin's family therapy approach to the second stage. (p. 272)

11. Describe a cognitive-behavioural approach to treatment of bulimia. Include description of both behavioural methods (to alter actual eating) and cognitive methods (to alter beliefs). (p. 272)

12. Describe Canadian eating disorder prevention programs. (p. 274)

SELF-TEST, CHAPTER 9

(* Items not covered in Study Questions.)

MULTIPLE CHOICE

1. Individuals with anorexia nervosa
   a. stop eating because of an abnormal increase in blood sugar, which alters their perceptions of hunger.
   b. fear gaining weight so much that they stop eating.
   c. have lost their appetite, leading them to stop eating.
   d. stop eating but do not lose weight.

2. Distorted body image in anorexics is often manifested by
   a. extreme avoidance of mirrors and scales.
   b. critical evaluation of body areas such as stomach and buttocks.
   c. frequent questioning of others regarding their appearance.
   d. checking behaviours designed to ensure that their stomach and buttocks appear smaller than in reality.

3. Canadian studies on the incidence of eating disorders suggest that
   a. bulimia is more common than anorexia among adolescents.
   b. the lifetime rate for females having an eating disorder is 1.6 percent.
   c. many females may not meet the existing diagnostic criteria for an eating disorder but may show signs of vulnerability to these disorders.
   d. all of the above.
   e. none of the above.

4. What is the most likely prognosis for a person with anorexia nervosa?
   a. regain normal weight as they enter puberty
   b. develop bulimia nervosa
   c. enter treatment and maintain normal weight following treatment
   d. recovery, for 70 percent of those that are treated

5. Compared to the binge, purging is felt by many bulimics to be
   a. a source of relief.
   b. more anxiety producing.
   c. more disgusting.
   d. a source of pride.

6. Which brain structure has been hypothesized to play a role in eating disorders?
   a. frontal lobe
   b. hippocampus
   c. hypothalamus
   d. pituitary gland

7.   The incidence of eating disorders has been rising steadily since the 1950s. This provides the best evidence for the _____ theory of eating disorder.

   a.   biological
   b.   socio-cultural
   c.   psychodynamic
   d.   family systems

8.   Studies of the personality of anorexics indicate that they are generally

   a.   impulsive, adventurous, outgoing.
   b.   confused, disoriented, withdrawn.
   c.   shy, obedient, perfectionistic.
   d.   warm, sensitive, helpful.

9.   In the cognitive-behavioural view, the non-eating of anorexics is reinforced by

   a.   reducing anxiety about being fat.
   b.   reducing sexual demands from males.
   c.   attention of overly concerned family members.
   d.   increased time and energy for studies.

10.   The first step in treating anorexia nervosa is

   a.   medication to reduce anxiety about eating.
   b.   education on the importance of a well balanced diet.
   c.   hospitalization to promote and monitor eating.
   d.   assessment to identify causes and plan individualized treatment.

11.   The _____ Approach is a labour-intensive method that recruits parents and requires them to find creative ways to feed their children and restore them to a healthy weight. Parents are taught that they are not to blame; but at the same time, they are taught to be supportive and not critical.

   a.   Minuchin
   b.   Maudsley
   c.   Freudian
   d.   Weight Watchers

12.   A factor that distinguishes Canadian prevention programs is

   a.   the payment of costs by government health programs.
   b.   the high success rates.
   c.   the low success rates.
   d.   the active role taken by the target audience in the process.

SHORT ANSWER

1.   What are some physical effects of bulimia nervosa purging type?

2.   What are several characteristics of bulimic women in addition to eating patterns?

3.   Is there a genetic diathesis for eating disorders? Explain.

4.   How do cross-cultural data indicate the role of social/cultural factors in eating disorders?

5.   Summarize Bruch's psychodynamic view of eating disorders.

6.   Summarize a family systems model of the cause of eating disorders.

7.   Describe the hypothesized role of narcissism and perfectionism as personality factors in the etiology of eating disorders.

8.   What has research shown about the families of individuals with eating disorders?

9.   Describe the effectiveness of biological treatments for eating disorders.

10.   Describe cognitive methods to alter the beliefs of bulimics.

11.   Describe the two treatment implications of Fairburn's cognitive-behavioural theory of the maintenance of anorexia nervosa.

12.   Describe cognitive-behavioural methods to alter the actual eating behaviour of bulimics.

ANSWERS TO SELF-TEST, CHAPTER 9

MULTIPLE CHOICE

1. b (p. 256)   2. b (p. 256)   3. d (p. 257)   4. d (p. 258)
5. a (p. 259)   6. c (p. 262)   7. b (p. 263)   8. c (p. 267)
9. a (p. 270)   10. c (p. 271)   11. b (p. 272)   12. d (p. 274)

SHORT ANSWER

1. Frequent purging can change electrolyte balances, pronote tooth decay from stomach acid, cause swelling of the salivary glands, cause lung infections through inhaled food particles, etc. (p. 259)

2. They are depression, anxiety, and personality disorders. Problems with stealing and promiscuity suggest impulsiveness. (p. 259)

3. Eating disorders are four times more likely in close relatives. There is higher concordance in MZ than in DZ twins. These factors suggest a genetic diathesis although adoptee studies have not been done. (p. 262)

4. Eating disorders appear more prevalent in industrialized countries, where there is a social emphasis on thinness, although evidence is lacking. (p. 264)

5. Parents who impose wishes on a child ignoring the child's desires, raise that child to feel ineffectual. The child does not learn to recognize internal needs (like hunger) and seizes on societal emphasis on thinness as way to be in control and have an identity. (p. 267)

6. Minuchin has proposed that eating disorders play the role of helping families avoid other conflicts. He documented that families of children with eating disorders are characterized by enmeshment, overprotectiveness, rigidity, and lack of conflict resolution. However, the causal relationship between these characteristics and the eating disorder has not been established; starvation itself can cause profound changes in personality. (p. 267)

7. Steiger et al. has suggested that patients with eating disorders have high levels of narcissism, even in remission. Perfectionism is believed to be highly relevant to an understanding of eating disorders. A variety of studies have found a positive correlation between scores on scales of perfectionism and severity of eating disorder. (p. 267)

8. Family research has produced confusing results. The patients report family conflict, but the parents do not. There is some evidence of disturbed family relations, but these behaviours don't fit theories and are unclear as they are based on reports, not observations. (p. 267)

9. Drugs have not proven effective in anorexia. Depressed bulimics are helped by antidepressants, although many drop out and effects last only as long as drug is taken. (p. 271)

10. Patients are urged to identify, question, and change beliefs that weight is vital to acceptance by self and others and that only extreme dieting can control weight. (p. 272)

11. Fairburn suggests that self-control should be a principal focus of treatment, while traditional issues such as self-esteem and interpersonal relations need not be addressed in therapy. He also suggests that clients can be shifted away from achieving satisfaction from controlling eating to a sense of achievement in other activities. (p. 272)

12. The client brings "forbidden" food to session and eats with relaxation and coaching to not purge. The client discusses thoughts and feelings while actually eating and is urged to eat normal well-balanced meals. (p. 272)

Chapter 10 Mood Disorders

OVERVIEW

The previous four chapters covered a wide range of problems related, in one way or another, to anxiety and stress. They included both psychological disorders and medical conditions in which anxiety and stress are prominent.

The next two chapters discuss two groups of disorders in which physiological factors have been widely studied. They are mood disorders, such as depression and schizophrenia. Complex, yet similar, physiological theories involving neurotransmitters (commonly known as brain imbalances) have been developed for both disorders.

Chapter 10 covers mood disorders, including lowered mood (depression) and heightened mood (mania). It also discusses suicide, which is often associated with depression. The literature on mood disorders is complex. Physiological and genetic factors have been studied for a long time, both because drugs are effective in treating them and because manic individuals experience rapid mood shifts that often seem otherwise inexplicable. Psychological research has also been extensive and psychological therapies have proven effective.

For similar reasons, physiological and genetic factors have long been suspected in schizophrenia (Chapter 11). Schizophrenia has been the subject of extensive research. It has been a difficult problem to understand and to treat. Drugs are a core part of treatment but are only partially effective.

After Chapters 10 and 11, the text shifts to disorders in which social and behavioural issues seem more prominent.

CHAPTER SUMMARY

The chapter begins by describing *General Characteristics of Mood Disorders*. DSM labels are based on the pattern and severity of depressive and manic episodes. Individuals with very different or heterogeneous behaviours receive the same label, suggesting other distinctions may be important.

Psychological Theories of Mood Disorders are well developed and varied. Psychoanalytic theory suggests that dependent people remain stuck in sadness because they cannot work through the anger that all people experience following a loss. Beck's cognitive theory suggests that depressives understand events through cognitive distortions that lead them to blame themselves for negative outcomes. Helplessness/hopelessness theory suggests that difficulty controlling negative events leads people to attribute the difficulty to themselves and feel hopeless about influencing outcomes, thereby resulting in depression. The interpersonal approach suggests that depressed individuals have fewer social supports, perhaps because their ineffective behaviours lead others to avoid them. Theories of mania are less well developed but view mania as a defence against depressing ideas about self.

Biological Theories of Mood Disorders are important because of genetic predisposition, especially for bipolar disorders. Research indicates that depressives and manics have difficulty with certain brain neurotransmitters; however, the nature of this difficulty is unclear. Neuroendocrine difficulties are also suggested.

Therapies for Mood Disorders include psychotherapeutic approaches derived from psychological theories of depression, as well as somatic treatments, including drugs and electroconvulsive shock treatment. Considerable research has studied the relative effectiveness and utility of these approaches.

Suicide is partially related to depression, although many suicidal individuals are not obviously depressed or otherwise disordered. The text reviews basic facts and theories, describes approaches to preventing suicide, and discusses ethical issues in dealing with suicide. The unique problems of Canada's Aboriginal peoples with regard to suicide are considered.

ESSENTIAL CONCEPTS

1. *DSM–IV* lists two major mood disorders (major depression and bipolar disorder) and two chronic mood disorders (dysthymic and cyclothymic disorder).

2. Depression occurs about twice as often in women as men. Differences in cognitive styles, types of stressors the two groups encounter, and rates of victimization are being explored as causes.

3. Freud proposed that orally fixated people who experience a loss are unable to accept the anger that results such that they do not stop grieving and become depressed.

4. Beck suggests that depression results from cognitive schemata involving negative views of the self, the world, and the future.

5. The learned helplessness theory of depression evolved out of research that found depressive-like behaviours in animals exposed to inescapable aversive events. The current version emphasizes feelings of hopelessness that result from self-blame for aversive events.

6. Interpersonal approaches note that depressed people have fewer social supports, perhaps because their behaviours lead others to avoid them.

7. There is little psychological theorizing regarding bipolar disorder. Generally, mania is seen as a defence against depression or similar states.

8. Genetic data indicate there is a heritable component to major mood disorders, especially bipolar disorder.

9. Biological theories developed out of drug research and suggest problems with certain neurotransmitters or with hormones secreted in the brain.

10. Physiological and psychological theories of depression are probably two different ways to describe the same phenomenon.

11. Beck's cognitive therapy has been widely studied for treating depression.

12. There are several biological treatments for depression, including electroconvulsive therapy and antidepressant drugs. Lithium is a useful drug in treating bipolar disorder. Some approaches can have serious side effects.

13. While not all people who commit suicide are depressed, many people who are depressed think about or attempt taking their own life.

14. Suicide prevention centres have developed methods to help people who are considering suicide.

15. Traditionally, therapists have devoted themselves to preventing suicide, although this can raise quality-of-life issues. More recent debates over physician-assisted suicide raise additional issues.

KEY TERMS

altruistic suicide (p.)

depressive paradox (p. 297)

anomic suicide (p. 314)

depressive predictive certainty (p. 298)

attribution (p. 297)

double depression (p. 290)

autonomy (p. 293)

dysthymic disorder (p. 290)

bilateral ECT (p. 307)

egoistic suicide (p. 314)

bipolar I disorder (p. 285)

electroconvulsive therapy (ECT) (p. 307)

bipolar II disorder (p. 287)

hypomania (p. 287)

brooding (p. 284)

kindling hypothesis (p. 284)

congruency hypothesis (p. 294)

learned helplessness theory (p. 296)

cyclothymic disorder (p. 290)

lithium carbonate (p. 310)

depression (p. 281)

major depressive disorder (MDD) (p. 282)

mania (p. 281)   ruminative coping (p. 284)

monoamine oxidase (MAO) inhibitors (p. 300)   seasonal affective disorder (SAD) (p. 289)

mood disorders (p. 281)   sociotropy (p. 293)

negative triad (p. 291)   Stroop task (p. 292)

phototherapy (p. 310)   suicide prevention centres (p. 318)

postpartum depression (p. 288)   tricyclic drugs (p. 300)

psychologizer (p. 281)   unilateral ECT (p. 307)

Study Questions

GENERAL CHARACTERISTICS OF MOOD DISORDERS (p. 281)

1.   Give at least five different general characteristics of depression and of mania. (p. 281) Distinguish between the two major mood disorders (p. 285) and the two chronic mood disorders (p. 290) in *DSM–IV*. Discuss the prevalence of major depression and bipolar disorder in the Canadian population. (p. 285) What is meant by "within the categories"? (p. 287) Discuss the incidence and possible causes of postpartum depression, based on recent Canadian studies. (p. 288)

PSYCHOLOGICAL THEORIES OF MOOD DISORDERS (p. 290)

2.   Describe the psychoanalytic theory of (normal) bereavement. What childhood circumstances may cause bereavement to go astray and how? What is the current status of this theory? (p. 290)

3. Describe the three levels of cognitive activity that lead to depressed feelings, according to Beck. Evaluate this theory by describing research on two points. (p. 291) Summarize the findings of recent Canadian studies designed to test predictions based on Beck's schema notion. Discuss Canadian research on personality orientations in depression. (p. 293)

4. Describe three stages in the evolution of the helplessness/hopelessness theory of depression. What five problems remain? (p. 296)

5. Summarize an interpersonal theory of depression by describing five interpersonal characteristics of depressed individuals. According to research, do these characteristics lead to depression, result from depression, or both? (p. 298)

6. How have most psychological theories viewed the two phases of bipolar disorder? Describe a study suggesting that manics try to conceal low self-esteem. (p. 299)

BIOLOGICAL THEORIES OF MOOD DISORDERS (p. 299)

7. What three research areas suggest biological factors in mood disorders? What has genetic research found regarding inheritance of bipolar depression? of unipolar depression? (p. 299)

8. What are the theorized roles of norepinephrine and serotonin in mania and in depression? Describe the drug actions that led to these theories. Describe two research approaches used to evaluate these theories (and the limitation of each). Describe new findings regarding drug actions and how they have an impact on the theories. (p. 300)

9.   Which part of the neuroendocrine system has been linked to depression and how? What do the neurotransmitter and neuroendocrine findings suggest about psychological theories of depression? (p. 302)

THERAPIES FOR MOOD DISORDERS (p. 302)

10.   Regarding psychological therapies for depression, briefly describe two psychodynamic therapies, cognitive/behaviour therapy, and social skills training (p. 302). Describe the NIMH research program including its importance, the groups and procedures, seven findings, and one controversy. (p. 304) Describe three general goals of psychological treatment for bipolar disorder. (p. 306)

11.   Three biological therapies are discussed. For each, describe its effectiveness, advantages, and disadvantages. (p. 306)

SUICIDE (p. 310)

12.   Discuss the epidemiology of suicide in Canada. (p. 311) Discuss the rates and causes of suicide in Aboriginal (First Nations) communities in Canada. (p. 312 and 318)

13.   Discuss the relationship between psychological disorders and suicide. (p. 312)

14.   Describe four theories of suicide. According to psychological tests, what are three characteristics of people likely to and people not likely to commit suicide? List two reasons why it is difficult to predict suicide in individual cases. (p. 313)

15. Summarize Shneidman's approach to suicide prevention and the general approach of suicide prevention centres. What clinical and ethical issues do health professionals face in preventing suicide and in assisting suicide? (p. 318)

SELF-TEST, CHAPTER 10

(* Items not covered in Study Questions.)

MULTIPLE CHOICE

1. Vanessa reported feeling a lack of energy, difficulty sleeping, not eating, difficulty concentrating, and a loss of interest in activities she previously enjoyed. Which of the following is the most likely diagnosis for Vanessa?
   a. eating disorder
   b. major depression
   c. bipolar disorder
   d. generalized anxiety disorder

2. Jack reports being in a wonderful mood. He has been very active at work lately, even working far into the night, as he seems to need only a few hours of sleep. He is very talkative and quickly moves from one topic to another, describing a scheme he has for making a fortune in the stock market. Which of the following diagnoses best fits Jack?
   a. overanxious disorder
   b. dysthymic disorder
   c. bipolar disorder
   d. None of the above. Jack does not fit the criteria for a mental disorder.

3. According to Canadian epidemiological research, people at risk for MDD are those who
   a. are female.
   b. have separated from a partner within the last year.
   c. have a low income.
   d. all of the above.

4. Iris has been feeling depressed most of the time for the past three years. She generally feels inadequate, sleeps a great deal, has trouble concentrating, and avoids social contact. The most likely diagnosis for Iris would be
   a. cyclothymic disorder.
   b. bipolar I disorder.
   c. dysthymic disorder.
   d. hypomania.

5.   Which of the following is not suggested in the textbook as a possible explanation for the higher rate of depression in females over that of males?

    a.   Females may experience different stressors than males due to different roles.

    b.   Females are more likely to be victimized than males.

    c.   Females often adopt a more ruminative coping style than males.

    d.   All of the above.

    e.   None of the above.

6.   According to Freud's theory, a depressed person is fixated in the oral stage of development which causes them to become

    a.   dependent on other people for the maintenance of self-esteem.

    b.   angry at other people because of their need for self-esteem.

    c.   afraid of their dependence leading to repression.

    d.   none of the above.

7.   According to the cognitive theory of depression, depressive cognitive biases are

    a.   pessimistic global views of self, world, and future.

    b.   negative beliefs about how things work in the world.

    c.   negative schemata triggered by negative life events.

    d.   distorted ways of reaching conclusions about events.

8.   Which of the following is a key idea in interpersonal theories of depression?

    a.   Depressive behaviours are reinforced by others seeking to cheer up the individual.

    b.   Interpersonal trauma leads to withdrawal and depression.

    c.   Depressed people withdraw from social contact and, over time, lose social skills.

    d.   Poor social skills both lead to and result from depression.

*9.   Iceland is as dark in the winter as Canada, but Icelanders suffer SAD at a much lower rate. Which of the following has been suggested as a possible explanation for this difference?

    a.   Icelanders may have adapted genetically so that they are relatively protected from SAD.

    b.   Canadian winters, while as dark, are much more severe than those of Iceland.

    c.   Canada has many more individuals living at very low socio-economic levels.

    d.   None of the above.

10.   Which of the following has not been a major finding from Canadian studies on personality orientation in depression?

    a.   Perfectionistic individuals tend to experience relapse when confronted with achievement-related stressors.

    b.   A significant amount of support was found for the "congruency hypothesis."

    c.   Self criticism may be associated with negative interpersonal cycles that characterize troubled relationships.

    d.   All of the above.

    e.   None of the above.

11. Research investigating the effects of medication on depression has recently been focusing on
    a. how side effects of the medication play a role in the reduction of depression.
    b. the effects on the postsynaptic site during medication trials.
    c. glucose metabolism changes due to medication withdrawal.
    d. the joint effects of hormonal regulation and medication administration.

12. Which of the following describes the relationship between depression and suicide?
    a. Almost all people who commit suicide are depressed.
    b. Almost all people who are depressed attempt suicide.
    c. Although depressed people often attempt suicide, many suicides are committed by people who are not depressed.
    d. Contrary to popular belief, there is no relationship between depression and suicide.

13. A businessman commits suicide when he must file for bankruptcy. According to Durkheim, this is which type of suicide?
    a. altruistic
    b. egoistic
    c. intrinsic
    d. anomic

SHORT ANSWER

1. List five characteristics of depression in addition to feeling sad.

2. Discuss the findings of Canadian research with regard to other health issues in individuals with bipolar disorder.

3. Summarize recent Canadian findings on the nature of postpartum depression.

4. Discuss the main results of Canadian research designed to test Beck's theory of etiology of depression.

5. Summarize the current version of the helplessness theory of depression.

6. Discuss recent findings about gender differences in coping with depression.

7. Describe a study suggesting that manics try to conceal low self-esteem.

8. Describe two strategies used in research on the relationship between neurotransmitters and depression.

9. How is the neuroendocrine system linked to depression?

10. What do therapists do to treat depression, based on cognitive theories of its cause?

11. Identify one advantage and one disadvantage to drug treatment for serious depression.

12. Discuss the general model of the causes of suicidal behaviour as summarized in the 2006 Government of Canada report on mental health and mental illness in Canada.

13. Describe Shneidman's approach to suicide prevention.

14. Describe factors identified by Survival for Tribal People as likely causes of the high suicide rate among Canadian Aboriginal peoples.

ANSWERS TO SELF-TEST, CHAPTER 10

MULTIPLE CHOICE

1. b (p. 282)   2. c (p. 285)   3. d (p. 285)   4. c (p. 290)
5. d (p. 283)   6. a (p. 290)   7. a (p. 291)   8. d (p. 298)
9. a (p. 290)   10. b (p. 293)   11. b (p. 306)   12. c (p. 310)
13. d (p. 313)

SHORT ANSWER

1. Change in sleep, eating, activity. Loss of interest, concentration, and energy. Social withdrawal. Negative feelings about self. Thoughts of suicide. (p. 282)

2. Rates of chronic fatigue syndrome, migraine, asthma, chronic bronchitis, multiple chemical sensitivities, hypertension, and gastric ulcer were high in people with bipolar disorder (compared with a reference group). (p. 286)

3. Canadian researchers suggest that the onset of postpartum depression can be predicted by levels of depression in the pregnancy period, as well as lack of warmth and care from caregivers in childhood. They also found links with lower socio-economic status and other forms of stress. A particularly important stressor can be a difficult, irritable infant. (p. 288)

4. Canadian research into the validity of Beck's model of the etiology of depression suggests that there are cognitive differences between depressed and non-depressed individuals. The former endorse more negative descriptions of themselves, pay greater attention to negative stimuli, and can access negative information more readily than the latter. In addition, depressed individuals have reduced accessibility to positive information about themselves and can more easily be induced to a negative mood state. (p. 291)

5. The current theory emphasizes hopelessness. Individuals have low self-esteem and attribute negative experiences to factors which are internal, stable, and global. Thus, they feel hopeless. (p. 296)

6. Nolen-Hoeksema and her associates have focused on gender differences in ruminative coping versus distraction when people experience feelings of depression. Females are more likely than males to engage in ruminative coping. Males are more likely to rely on distraction and doing something that diverts their attention (e.g., engaging in physical activity, watching television). (p. 283)

7. Manics reported good self-esteem but showed poor self-esteem on an indirect test (inferring esteem of the character in a short story). (p. 297)

8. (a) The study of metabolic by-products of neurotransmitters in the blood, urine, etc. (b) The study of whether drugs that influence neurotransmitters also influence the disorders. (p. 300)

9. The neuroendocrine system consists of brain areas (hypothalamus, etc.) that release hormones, which influence depression-related behaviours such as appetite and sleep. Overactivity in these areas could be part of depression. (p. 302)

10. They help clients identify and change their beliefs using logical analysis, providing contrary examples or experiences, etc. (p. 303)

11. Advantage: they hasten recovery. Disadvantages: drug side effects, relapse common if drug is discontinued. (p. 306)

12. This model, which is recommended as a guide for suicide prevention programs, includes four categories of relevant factors: predisposing factors, precipitating factors, contributing factors, and protective factors. (p. 314)

13. Shneidman emphasizes helping them to find and consider other alternatives (also to reduce suffering and to reconsider suicide). (p. 315)

14. The rights group Survival For Tribal Peoples suggests that loss of cultural identity, industrial development, and depletion of natural resources are among factors that contribute to the high suicide rate among Canada's Aboriginal peoples. (p. 317)

Chapter 11 Schizophrenia

OVERVIEW

Chapters 10 and 11 discuss two disorders that have been the subject of extensive research. Similar physiological theories have developed implicating brain neurotransmitters in both disorders. Mood disorders (Chapter 10) have been the subject of extensive psychological and physiological research, with effective treatments emerging from both areas. Schizophrenia (Chapter 11) has led to even more extensive study, at least in part because no overt cure exists.

Of all the disorders covered in the text, schizophrenia comes closest to the common understanding of being "crazy." Despite extensive study, it remains a major concern both socially and scientifically. Historically, psychopathologists have disagreed on how to define schizophrenia and even on whether the term refers to one or to several different problems. Despite recent advances, no cure for schizophrenia has emerged. Currently, a combination of approaches emphasizing drugs can manage, but not cure, the problem. Schizophrenics are a major portion of patients in mental hospitals and health clinics.

After Chapter 11, the focus of the text shifts to disorders that often seem more social and behavioural in nature. These include substance abuse and dependence disorders (Chapter 12), personality disorders including anti-social personality disorder (Chapter 13), and sexual and gender identity disorders (Chapter 14).

CHAPTER SUMMARY

Schizophrenia is a complex disorder that is difficult to define. What we currently define as one disorder may in fact be several similar disorders. The *Clinical Symptoms of Schizophrenia* include positive symptoms (or behavioural excesses, such as confused thinking and speaking) and negative symptoms (or behavioural deficits, including lack of energy, interest, and feelings).

The History of the Concept of Schizophrenia has included two traditions. Many American ideas about schizophrenia developed out of Bleuler's broad, psychoanalytically-based definition. Recent DSM editions have moved toward Kraepelin's narrower, descriptive (rather than theoretical) approach, which has always been popular in Europe. Currently, *DSM-IV-TR* recognizes three subcategories of schizophrenia. Disorganized schizophrenics exhibit blatantly bizarre and silly behaviours. Catatonic schizophrenics show primarily motor symptoms, including wild excitement and apathetic withdrawal to the point of immobility. Paranoid schizophrenics have well-organized delusions of persecution, grandiosity, and jealousy. Current research suggests the distinction between positive and negative symptoms represents another useful way to subcategorize schizophrenia. Comorbid conditions appear to play a role in the development, severity, and course of schizophrenia. Comorbid substance abuse is a major problem for patients with schizophrenia, occurring in as many as 70 percent of them.

Research on the Etiology of Schizophrenia has been extensive. Genetic, biochemical, and neurological data strongly suggest a biological diathesis to schizophrenia. Genetic data from family, twin, and more sophisticated adoptee studies all point to a genetic predisposition to schizophrenia. While schizophrenia is likely not caused by one gene, conventional gene linkage and association analyses point to the possible role of numerous specific genes. Biochemical research suggests that for some schizophrenics there is excessive activity in nerve tracts of the brain that utilize the neurotransmitter dopamine. New neurological techniques suggest brain atrophy in schizophrenics with negative symptoms. Prenatal infections may be involved for these individuals.

Other research has looked at social class, family, and other variables. Since schizophrenia runs in families, it is possible to select and follow children with a high risk of becoming schizophrenic. These studies suggest stressors that may potentiate the diatheses suggested by biological research.

Many biological and psychological *Therapies for Schizophrenia* have been attempted. Antipsychotic drugs were a major advance. However, schizophrenics need additional help to cope with social living. Traditional psychotherapeutic approaches have not been very effective with schizophrenics, but family and behavioural methods show promise. There remains a need to integrate skills and knowledge of various disciplines in order to help schizophrenics lead as normal a life as possible.

ESSENTIAL CONCEPTS

1. Most symptoms of schizophrenia can be grouped as either positive symptoms (or behavioural excesses, such as confused thinking and speaking) or negative symptoms (or behavioural deficits, including lack of energy, interest, and feelings).

2. Historic definitions of schizophrenia include Kraepelin's concept of dementia praecox and Bleuler's concept of loose associative threads. Currently, *DSM-IV-TR* has moved to Kraepelin's narrower definition.

3. *DSM-IV-TR* defines three major subcategories of schizophrenia: disorganized, catatonic, and paranoid. These subcategories are limited. Research suggests the distinction between positive and negative symptoms may provide more useful distinctions.

4. Evidence from family, twin, and adoptee studies indicates a substantial genetic diathesis to schizophrenia, although this alone cannot fully explain the disorder's etiology.

5. Extensive research links schizophrenia to dopamine activity in particular brain tracts and abnormalities in the prefrontal cortex. The evidence suggests that both genetic and prenatal factors may lead to dopamine tract changes. Newer drugs used in treating schizophrenia implicate other neurotransmitters, such as serotonin, in the disorder.

6. There is a link between low social status and schizophrenia. Sociogenic and social-selection explanations have been offered for this correlation.

7. Early theories that family issues cause schizophrenia have been discredited. However, family patterns of communication and emotional expression may affect the post-hospital adjustment of schizophrenics.

8. Biochemical research suggests that increased sensitivity of dopamine receptors in the limbic area of the brain is related to the positive symptoms of schizophrenia; negative symptoms may be due to dopamine underactivity in the prefrontal cortex. Recently, the role of glutamate receptors is being investigated as one of the variables involved in the cause of this disorder.

9.   The brains of schizophrenics, especially those with negative symptoms, have enlarged ventricles and prefrontal atrophies, as well as abnormalities in the temporal and limbic areas. Viral infections during the second trimester of fetal development may be the cause of these abnormalities.

10.   Children of schizophrenic patients have been studied longitudinally in high-risk projects that shed light on the etiology of schizophrenia.

11.   Currently, no treatments of schizophrenia are totally effective. Neuroleptic medications are effective in controlling the positive symptoms of schizophrenia for many patients, but not the negative symptoms.

12.   Family therapy and behavioural approaches show promise in improving the social adjustment of schizophrenics.

13.   Well-organized community programs can assist schizophrenic patients in their attempts at independent living.

14.   There remains a need to integrate skills of many disciplines to better help schizophrenics.

KEY TERMS

alogia (p. 329)

delusional disorder (p. 333)

anhedonia (p. 329)

delusional jealousy (p. 333)

antipsychotic drugs (p. 349)

delusions (p. 327)

asociality (p. 330)

dementia praecox (p. 331)

avolition (p. 329)

disorganized schizophrenia (p. 333)

catatonic immobility (p. 330)

disorganized speech (thought disorder) (p. 327)

catatonic schizophrenia (p. 333)

dopamine theory (p. 339)

cognitive enhancement therapy (CET) (p. 357)

expressed emotion (EE) (p. 345)

flat affect (p. 330)

personal therapy (p. 356)

grandiose delusions (p. 333)

positive symptoms (p. 327)

group homes (p. 364)

prefrontal lobotomy (p. 349)

halfway houses (p. 364)

residual schizophrenia (p. 334)

hallucinations (p. 328)

schizophrenia (p. 325)

ideas of reference (p. 333)

schizophrenogenic mother (p. 345)

inappropriate affect (p. 330)

social-selection theory (p. 344)

incoherence (p. 327)

sociogenic hypothesis (p. 344)

loose associations (derailment) (p. 327)

undifferentiated schizophrenia (p. 334)

negative symptoms (p. 329)

waxy flexibility (p. 330)

paranoid schizophrenia (p. 333)

STUDY QUESTIONS

CLINICAL SYMPTOMS OF SCHIZOPHRENIA (p. 326)

1. Summarize the symptoms of schizophrenia, including three positive symptoms and five negative symptoms, plus two others. Give examples of the various terms explaining why they are positive or negative symptoms. (p. 326)

HISTORY OF THE CONCEPT (p. 331)

2. Describe Kraepelin's and Bleuler's early views on schizophrenia. Trace the way Bleuler's view broadened in America. List five ways in which the newer *DSM-TR* definitions of schizophrenia have moved toward the narrower European view. (p. 331)

3. Summarize several distinguishing characteristics of each of the three subtypes of schizophrenia in *DSM-IV-TR*. Evaluate these subtypes by describing (a) their limitations and (b) evolving interest in another approach to subdividing schizophrenia. (p. 332)

4. List the five subtypes of schizophrenia identified by the Henrichs and Awad (1993) thorough cluster analysis of the scores of a battery of neuropsychological tests. (p. 334)

ETIOLOGY OF SCHIZOPHRENIA (p. 335)

5. Describe and evaluate three approaches to studying genetic factors in schizophrenia. Summarize the overall importance of genetic factors. (p. 335)

6. Why does genetic evidence suggest the need to study biochemical factors in schizophrenia? Summarize three findings indicating that dopamine activity is a factor in schizophrenia. Summarize current views on (a) dopamine levels vs. dopamine receptors and (b) positive vs. negative symptoms. How could different neural pathways allow prefrontal underactivity to affect both negative symptoms and, indirectly, positive symptoms? Identify three weaknesses to current dopamine theory and two other chemicals that may be involved. (p. 337)

7. Summarize data implicating (a) enlarged ventricles and (b) the prefrontal cortex in schizophrenia. What suggests that these differences are not purely genetic? Summarize data suggesting they may result from (a) birth complications or (b) viral infection before birth. (p. 341)

8. What is the relationship between social class and schizophrenia? What does it mean to say this is not a "continuous progression"? Describe two theories of this relationship and a recent Israeli study comparing them. (p. 344)

9. According to research, what family patterns may contribute to schizophrenia and influence the post-hospitalization adjustment of schizophrenics? What is the advantage of "high-risk" studies in studying the development of schizophrenia? What have these studies found, especially regarding positive and negative symptoms? (p. 346)

10. How do "high-risk" studies suggest a different etiology for schizophrenia, one that involves predominately positive symptoms vs. a form that involves predominately negative symptoms? (p. 346)

THERAPIES FOR SCHIZOPHRENIA (p. 347)

11. Why were earlier biological treatments abandoned? What are the benefits and the problems of antipsychotic drugs? What is current clinical practice regarding their use? How did the introduction of clozapine stimulate change? (p. 349)

12. The text describes three general psychological treatment approaches and three recent cognitive-behavioural approaches. For each, describe the (a) rationale, (b) method, and (c) results, if any. Summarize the origins and rationale of case management. (p. 355)

13. Summarize the general methods used by the PRIME Clinic. (p. 360)

14. Discuss the new CAMH model. (p. 363)

SELF-TEST, CHAPTER 11

(* Items not covered in Study Questions.)

MULTIPLE CHOICE

*1.   Which of the following is required in order to make a diagnosis of schizophrenia?
   a.   hallucinations
   b.   disorganized speech
   c.   delusions
   d.   none of the above

2.   Formal thought disorder in schizophrenia refers to
   a.   delusions.
   b.   anhedonia.
   c.   disorganized speech.
   d.   hallucinations.

3.   Which of the following are examples of negative symptoms of schizophrenia?
   a.   blunted emotions, lack of initiative
   b.   hallucinations and delusions
   c.   difficulty concentrating, low intelligence, poor memory
   d.   catatonic immobility, waxy flexibility

4.   Which of the following are examples of positive symptoms of schizophrenia?
   a.   blunted emotions, lack of initiative
   b.   hallucinations and delusions
   c.   extreme optimism even in the face of major obstacles
   d.   catatonic immobility, waxy flexibility

5.   Mr. Hart spends long hours sitting in a chair with his arms behind his back and his left leg tucked under. No matter what is going on around him, he remains in this position. This is an example of which symptom of schizophrenia?
   a.   somatic passivity
   b.   waxy flexibility
   c.   catatonic immobility
   d.   inappropriate affect

6.   Which of the following is not one of the subtypes identified by Heinrichs and Awad in the analysis of scores on neuropsychological tests?
   a.   executive subtype
   b.   motor subtype
   c.   catatonic subtype
   d.   one with intact cognition

7. Family studies of the genetic basis for schizophrenia look at
   a. the rate of schizophrenia in relatives of schizophrenic patients.
   b. concordance for schizophrenia in cultures where incest is relatively common.
   c. the likelihood that a schizophrenic patient will have children.
   d. the effects of being raised by a schizophrenic parent.

8. Dopamine receptors appear responsible for
   a. primarily positive symptoms.
   b. primarily negative symptoms.
   c. the onset, but not the maintenance, of schizophrenia.
   d. the maintenance, but not the onset, of schizophrenia.

9. The social selection theory proposes that
   a. poverty causes schizophrenia.
   b. schizophrenia causes poverty.
   c. social discrimination causes both schizophrenia and poverty.
   d. poverty and schizophrenia are not related.

10. Data on expressed emotion (EE) indicate that schizophrenics are more likely to relapse (that is, return to the hospital) if their families
    a. are cool, calm, unemotional and aloof.
    b. are uninvolved.
    c. are critical and overinvolved with them.
    d. provide excessive emotional support and encouragement.

11. Extrapyramidal side effects primarily affect _____ functioning.
    a. visual
    b. auditory
    c. motor
    d. cognitive

12. Hogarty focuses on computer-based training in attention, memory, and problem solving, as well as social-cognitive skills (such as initiating conversations) in a process known as
    a. community monitoring.
    b. family therapy.
    c. behavioural-cognitive therapy.
    d. cognitive enhancement therapy.

13. Heinz Lehmann, a professor of psychiatry at McGill University, was involved in the discovery of which aspect of schizophrenia?
    a. the link between schizophrenia and influenza following WWI
    b. *Folie à Deux*
    c. the discovery of neuroleptics
    d. the genetic link with the etiology of schizophrenia

SHORT ANSWER

1. Describe five negative symptoms of schizophrenia.

2. What characteristics of the problem were emphasized by (a) Kraepelin's term "dementia praecox" and (b) Bleuler's term "schizophrenia?"

3. Why does *DSM-IV-TR's* definition of schizophrenia require that the patient have symptoms for at least six months?

4. John believes he has the instant answer to all the country's problems. When people avoid him (because he constantly lectures them on the topic), he decides they fear the president will hear his ideas and instantly implement them. The president happened to be in town, and John walked in on the meeting, assuming the president had come specifically to see him. When bodyguards threw him out, he became irate and declared the president was having sex with his wife and, thus, had refused to see him. What diagnosis is appropriate for John?

5. What has happened as a result of the low reliability of *DSM-IV* subcategories of schizophrenia?

6. Discuss the concept of comorbidity in schizophrenia.

7. Identify three weaknesses to the current dopamine theory of schizophrenia.

8. Why is it significant that schizophrenics may have enlarged ventricles?

9. Summarize data suggesting that viral complications contribute to neurological changes in schizophrenia.

10. Explain what the text means in saying that the relation between schizophrenia and social class is not a continuous progression.

11.   Describe what genetic counselling would involve based on recommendations of Hodgkins et al (2001) for families with schizophrenia.

12.   What do "case managers" do in treating schizophrenia and why?

ANSWERS TO SELF-TEST, CHAPTER 11

MULTIPLE CHOICE

1. d (p. 325)	2. c (p. 327)	3. a (p. 329)	4. b (p. 327)
5. c (p. 330)	6. c (p. 333)	7. a (p. 335)	8. a (p. 337)
9. b (p. 344)	10. c (p. 345)	11. c (p. 352)	12. d (p. 357)
13. c (p. 350)			

SHORT ANSWER

1.   Symptoms include (a) avolition or apathy, (b) alogia or slow and limited speech with little content, (c) anhedonia or not enjoying anything, (d) flat affect or lack of emotional response, (e) asociality or poor social skills and few friends. (p. 329)

2.   (a) Kraepelin emphasized early onset and progressive intellectual deterioration. (b) Bleuler emphasized underlying difficulty in thinking and communication. (p. 331)

3.   This was part of the move to a narrower, more Kraepelinian definition. People who abruptly develop symptoms typically recover within six months and, now, receive another diagnosis. (p. 332)

4.   Paranoid schizophrenia. (p. 333)

5.   There is much interest in finding better ways to subdivide schizophrenia, perhaps by distinguishing schizophrenics with positive, negative, and mixed symptoms. (p. 334)

6.   Comorbidity is a condition in which two or more conditions exist at the same time. Schizophrenia has shown significant comorbidity with substance abuse, depression, obsessive-compulsive disorder, post-traumatic stress disorder, and a variety of other psychotic symptoms. (p. 326)

7.   (a) Drugs block dopamine receptors quickly but take weeks to relieve symptoms. (b) To be effective, drugs must reduce dopamine to below normal. (c) Newer drugs affect other neurotransmitters. (p. 341)

8.   If ventricles (or brain openings) are enlarged, then the brain has shrunk. Evidence is that the loss is in subcortical areas, such as the prefrontal cortex. (p. 341)

9.   Schizophrenia was more common in people whose mothers were exposed to the influenza virus during their second trimester of pregnancy. (p. 342)

10.   Schizophrenia is decidedly (not just relatively) more common in the lowest social classes. (p. 344)

11.   Genetic counselling is a process of communication that involves conveying information about risk to patients and their relatives in order to assist them with making decisions about reproduction in light of the family data on genetic probabilities of offspring developing schizophrenia. (p. 366)

12.   They coordinate the services provided by a team and others in the community. Research shows that intensive, coordinated community services reduce hospitalization costs and improve adjustment in many areas. (p. 358)

Chapter 12 Substance-Related Disorders

OVERVIEW

The previous two chapters covered mood disorders and schizophrenia. Similar complex physiological theories have developed around both disorders. Physiological research and theory for the remaining disorders are not as extensive.

The next three chapters discuss disorders that have strong social and behavioural components. Chapter 12 discusses substance-related disorders, including abuse of alcohol, nicotine, marijuana, and hard drugs. Chapter 13 covers personality disorders, in which persistent and maladaptive personality traits or behaviours cause difficulty for the individual and others. The most well-known personality disorder is the anti-social personality or psychopath, characterized by anti-social behaviour and/or by lack of guilt over that behaviour. Chapter 14 discusses a wide range of disorders involving sexual behaviour.

Many of these problems involve behaviours that are maladaptive or socially unacceptable but not necessarily "disordered" in the traditional sense. Many are more bothersome to others than to the person involved. At times, it can be difficult to decide if they are psychological, legal, or moral/ethical problems. This can present dilemmas for treatment personnel.

The text's coverage of specific problems will conclude with Chapters 15 and 16, which deal with issues and disorders of childhood and old age.

CHAPTER SUMMARY

Drugs have always been used and abused to alter mood and consciousness. Contemporary practice distinguishes between substance abuse that affects daily functioning and substance dependence that also produces physiological changes leading to physical tolerance (or decreasing effects) and withdrawal reactions. The chapter describes effects of five groups of commonly abused substances.

Alcohol Abuse and Dependence is a widespread social problem. Alcohol produces short-term effects, including poor judgement and coordination, and long-term effects, including addiction and physical deterioration. Binge drinking is a serious problem in Canadian universities.

Nicotine and Cigarette Smoking is still common, despite strong evidence of health risks. *Marijuana* produces a "high" characterized by decreased cognitive and psychomotor functioning. Long-term use has physical and psychological effects. Debate continues over its possible uses in medical treatment.

Sedatives and Stimulants that respectively decrease and increase responsiveness, include several illegal and addictive drugs. *LSD and Other Hallucinogens* were originally studied, and are now abused, for their mind-altering properties. Only recently have several researchers begun to look at the therapeutic effects of several drugs labelled as hallucinogenic.

Research into The Etiology of Substance Abuse and Dependence has identified cultural, psychological, and biological variables; for example, individual beliefs about alcohol's effects as well as general personality variables influence alcohol's effects.

Therapy for Alcohol Abuse and Dependence includes detoxification, followed by several possible therapies, each of which is only modestly effective. Similarly, *Therapy for the Use of Illicit Drugs* via biological and/or psychological approaches is of limited effectiveness. *Treatment of Cigarette Smoking* describes psychological and biological treatments that are effective in smoking cessation; however, relapse is a major problem.

Prevention of Substance Abuse notes the social and pragmatic value of prevention programs, especially those directed at adolescents. That tobacco prevention programs, in particular, are common and effective methods is becoming apparent.

ESSENTIAL CONCEPTS

1. Substance abuse involves use of a drug to the extent that it interferes with functioning. Substance dependence involves more serious interference plus withdrawal reactions and increased tolerance.

2. Alcohol is an addicting drug that exacts a high cost from many individuals and from society.

3. Alcohol's short-term physiological effects are complex and are mediated by cognitive expectancies. The long-term consequences can be quite severe, both psychologically and biologically.

4. Inhalant abuse (the use of gasoline, household aerosol sprays, etc. to alter mood or consciousness) is a problem in some Canadian Native communities.

5. Cigarette smoking is a tremendous health problem for smokers, for those near them, and for society at large.

6. Marijuana interferes with cognitive functioning and psychomotor performance and appears to have some adverse physical effects with long-term use. Evidence for its medical and psychiatric use, while controversial, continues to grow. In Canada, because of Supreme Court rulings, people wishing to use marijuana for medical reasons can apply to be exempt from the federal ban on its use.

7. Sedatives or "downers" reduce the body's responsiveness. They include organic narcotics and synthetic barbiturates.

8. Sedatives are highly addicting and have important social consequences. For example, criminal behaviour may result from an addict's attempt to maintain the expensive habit.

9. Stimulants (amphetamines and cocaine) are "uppers" that heighten alertness and increase autonomic activity. They are considered addictive.

10. LSD and other hallucinogens produce a state that was once thought to mimic psychosis, characterized sometimes by dramatic changes in perception and cognition. Research is beginning to reveal psychiatric uses of hallucinogens, particularly in doses lower than those used for recreational purposes.

11.   Socia-cultural, psychological, and biological factors contribute to starting and continuing abuse.

12.   Current models of drug addiction suggest that all drugs with the ability to cause addiction do so by working on the same brain centres and neurotransmitters, primarily the brain's reward system which is facilitated by dopamine receptors.

13.   Therapy for alcohol and drug abuse usually begins with detoxification. Various biological and psychological therapies are difficult to evaluate but only modestly effective.

14.   Most ex-smokers quit spontaneously. Psychological and biological approaches are effective in the short run; however, relapse is an issue.

15.   Prevention remains the most effective approach to controlling substance abuse. Effective prevention programs are growing, especially in preventing tobacco use. The Canadian experience suggests that the more stringent and graphic the tobacco use warning, the more effective it is.

KEY TERMS

amphetamines (p. 383)

delirium tremens (DTs) (p. 368)

Antabuse (p. 393)

denormalization belief (p. 407)

barbiturates (p. 382)

detoxification (p. 393)

clonidine (p. 403)

Drug-Stroop Task (p. 390)

cocaine (p. 383)

ecstasy (p. 386)

conditioning theory of tolerance (p. 392)

feedforward mechanisms (p. 392)

controlled drinking (p. 397)

fetal alcohol syndrome (p. 374)

covert sensitization (p. 397)

flashback (p. 386)

cross-dependent (p. 402)

guided self-change (p. 398)

hallucinogen (p. 385)   nicotine (p. 375)

harm reduction therapy (p. 397)   opiates (p. 381)

hashish (p. 378)   opium (p. 381)

heroin (p. 381)   polydrug abuse (p. 369)

heroin antagonists (p. 402)   psilocybin (p. 385)

heroin substitutes (p. 402)   second-hand smoke (p. 377)

LSD (p. 385)   sedatives (p. 381)

marijuana (p. 378)   stimulants (p. 383)

mescaline (p. 385)   substance abuse (p. 368)

methadone (p. 402)   substance dependence (p. 368)

morphine (p. 381)   tolerance (p. 368)

motivational interviewing (p. 404)   withdrawal (p. 368)

STUDY QUESTIONS

1.   Identify and distinguish between substance dependence and substance abuse in *DSM-IV*. (p. 368)

ALCOHOL ABUSE AND DEPENDENCE (p. 368)

2. What are the indicators of alcohol dependence and alcohol abuse? (p. 368) Describe the Canadian data on binge drinking. (p. 371) Describe the short-term and long-term effects of alcohol abuse. (p. 373)

INHALANT USE DISORDERS (p. 375)

3. Describe why the abuse of inhalants is often considered a stepping stone to alcohol and drug abuse and how serious a problem it is in some Native communities in Canada. (p. 375)

NICOTINE AND CIGARETTE SMOKING (p. 375)

4. How prevalent and serious is smoking? What are the consequences of smoking, especially for nonsmokers? (p. 376)

MARIJUANA (p. 378)

5. Describe changes in prevalence of marijuana use. Describe the psychological, somatic, and therapeutic effects of marijuana. (p. 380)

6. Compare the overall effects of marijuana, an illegal drug, with those of tobacco and alcohol, both legal drugs. (p. 380)

SEDATIVES AND STIMULANTS (p. 381)

7.   The text identifies two groups of sedatives and two groups of stimulants. For each group, describe (a) short-term effects, (b) long-term effects, and (c) withdrawal effects. (p. 381)

LSD AND OTHER HALLUCINOGENS (p. 385)

8.   Summarize the history of LSD and other hallucinogens. What are the general effects of hallucinogens and what variables influence their effects? (p. 385)

ETIOLOGY OF SUBSTANCE ABUSE AND DEPENDENCE (p. 387)

9.   Why is the etiology of substance abuse and dependence a complex topic to study? Identify five socio-cultural variables affecting alcoholism and drug abuse (starting with cross-national variations). Describe three psychological variables (including three personality factors) affecting drug use. (p. 387)

10.   Summarize studies suggesting a biological diathesis for alcoholism. What may be the nature of this diathesis? (p. 391)

THERAPY FOR ALCOHOL ABUSE AND DEPENDENCE (p. 392)

11.   Why is admitting the problem often an issue with alcoholics? Describe and evaluate traditional hospital treatment of alcoholism. Briefly describe and evaluate five treatments for alcoholism (including three variations on cognitive-behavioural methods). Identify four general clinical considerations in treating alcoholics. (p. 392)

12. Discuss the philosophy and structure behind the treatment program of Poundmaker's Lodge. (p. 395)

THERAPY FOR THE USE OF ILLICIT DRUGS (p. 402)

13. Discuss the concept of harm reduction. (p. 397)

14. What is the central or first step in treating drug addiction? Describe and evaluate two biological and three psychological treatments for drug abuse. (p. 402)

TREATMENT OF CIGARETTE SMOKING (p. 404)

15. How do most people quit smoking? Illustrate the range of psychological treatments for smoking and discuss their effectiveness. Identify two biological treatments for smoking and discuss their effectiveness. What is relapse prevention? (p. 404)

PREVENTION OF SUBSTANCE ABUSE (p. 407)

16. Discuss the rationale of prevention programs generally. Describe seven common components of tobacco prevention programs (and note which one is counterproductive). (p. 407)

SELF-TEST, CHAPTER 12

(* Items not covered in Study Questions.)

MULTIPLE CHOICE

1.   Wanda drinks frequently and now does not require as much alcohol as six months ago to achieve the same effect. She reports that she can outdrink most people. Wanda is probably
   a.   genetically not predisposed to alcoholism.
   b.   developing a physiological dependence on alcohol.
   c.   acquiring behavioural skills in modulating her drinking.
   d.   deluding herself. This is not physically possible.

2.   When all costs and social damages are compared, the most damaging and costly drug in Canada is
   a.   heroin.
   b.   marijuana.
   c.   crack cocaine.
   d.   alcohol.

*3.   Most recent research on patterns of alcohol use suggests that
   a.   drinking is usually heaviest on weekends.
   b.   alcoholics typically alternate between binge episodes and relatively light drinking.
   c.   drinking follows well-demarcated stages.
   d.   there is no single pattern of alcohol abuse.

4.   Which of the following was not a finding of a survey of Canadian patterns of alcohol use among college students?
   a.   Very few, less than 15 percent, reported drinking five or more drinks on a single occasion since the start of the school year.
   b.   About 60 percent reported drinking five or more drinks on a single occasion since the start of the school year.
   c.   About 35 percent reported drinking eight or more drinks.
   d.   Men were more likely than women to have five or more drinks on a single occasion.

5.   Alcohol goes into the _____ and is absorbed into the blood, after which it is metabolized by the _____.
   a.   small intestine; kidneys
   b.   small intestine; liver
   c.   stomach; liver
   d.   stomach; kidneys

6.   Which of the following is not an inhalant that has been abused?
   a.   white-out correction fluid
   b.   spray paint
   c.   aerosol sprays
   d.   nitrous oxide in whipping cream cans
   e.   none of the above

*7.   Hashish is
   a.   derived from resin after smoking marijuana.
   b.   derived from resin from higher quality cannabis plants.
   c.   based upon a mixture of marijuana and heroin.
   d.   milder than marijuana.

8.   The benefit of marijuana when used for chronic illnesses is primarily
   a.   to reduce nausea for patients undergoing chemotherapy.
   b.   to increase immune function.
   c.   to improve attention and maintain medication adherence.
   d.   to prevent additional infection.

9.   Mark is experiencing the following symptoms after taking a drug: he feels an initial rush of ecstasy, has great self-confidence, and loses all his worries and fears. At the same time, he feels drowsy and relaxed. Which of the following drugs is Mark most likely to have taken recently?
   a.   heroin
   b.   alcohol
   c.   marijuana
   d.   cocaine

10.   An important socio-cultural variable that is cited in the increased use of cigarettes is
   a.   the role of the family in providing implicit messages regarding smoking.
   b.   rebound effects from the end of "just say no" campaigns.
   c.   the media and advertising.
   d.   the restriction of places where one may smoke.

11.   Although it has been shown that alcohol does not have a consistent effect upon stress, people continue to drink as a means to alleviate stress because
   a.   they expect it to help.
   b.   others suggest drinking to unwind.
   c.   drinking is more socially acceptable than consuming other drugs.
   d.   they are unaware of the severity of life stress they are experiencing.

12.   The treatment goal of Alcoholics Anonymous is
   a.   to cope with their spouse's or parent's drinking.
   b.   to change the public's perceptions of alcohol and alcoholism.
   c.   to learn to drink socially without becoming drunk.
   d.   complete abstinence from drinking.

13.   "Controlled drinking" refers to
   a.   using aversion therapy to control the drinking of alcoholics.
   b.   the approach to alcohol use promoted by Alcoholics Anonymous.
   c.   programs designed to teach alcoholics to drink in moderation rather than abstain completely.
   d.   preventing alcoholism through changes in society and laws such as prohibition.

SHORT ANSWER

1.   How serious a health problem is cigarette smoking?

2.   What are the withdrawal effects of opium-based narcotics?

3.   Describe one of the potential therapeutic uses of an hallucinogenic drug.

4.   Identify a number of socio-cultural variables in alcoholism.

5.   What is inherited as the genetic predisposition to alcoholism?

6.   Describe the difference between positive expectancies and negative expectancies in predicting drinking behaviour.

7.   Disulfiram or Antabuse can discourage alcoholics from drinking by . . .

8.   Briefly describe the philosophy of Poundmaker's Lodge.

9.   Describe how brief interventions that teach students how to drink can reduce alcohol consumption.

10.   What is the central or first step in treating drug addiction and why?

11.   What happens in self-help programs for drug addiction?

12.   How effective are biological treatments for cigarette smoking?

13.   Describe the savings that are projected for a national smoking prevention program in Canada.

ANSWERS TO SELF-TEST, CHAPTER 12

MULTIPLE CHOICE

1. b (p. 368)   2. d (p. 385)   3. d (p. 392)   4. a (p. 370)
5. b (p. 373)   6. e (p. 375)   7. b (p. 378)   8. a (p. 380)
9. a (p. 381)   10. c (p. 403)   11. a (p. 376)   12. d (p. 394)
13. c (p. 397)

SHORT ANSWER

1. Smoking accounts for 1 in 6 deaths and is the largest preventable cause of premature death. (p. 376)

2. Withdrawal effects resemble influenza and include sneezing, sweating, and (later) cramps, chills, sleeplessness. Diarrhea and vomiting may occur. (p. 382)

3. An investigation of nine OCD patients showed that when given psilocybin (the magic ingredient in "magic mushrooms"), the patients had substantial decreases in OCD symptoms, and these decreases tended to persist over time (Moreno, Wiegand, Taitano, & Delgado, 2006). Another investigation found substantial decreases in depressions believed to be treatment resistant when patients were administered ketamine. (p. 385)

4. Cross-cultural differences, availability, family, peer pressure, media. (p. 388)

5. People can inherit the ability to tolerate and drink large quantities of alcohol. (p. 391)

6. Positive expectancies are stronger predictors than negative expectancies of drinking behaviour. (p. 390)

7. They produce violent vomiting if one drinks alcohol after taking it. (p. 393)

8. Poundmaker's Lodge believes that in keeping with Native values, it is crucial to treat the entire person—spiritual, mental, emotional, and physical. The assumption is that the Aboriginal client will respond best to an approach that embraces both the philosophy of Alcoholics Anonymous (AA) or Narcotics Anonymous (NA) and Aboriginal cultural awareness. (p. 395)

9. Alan Marlatt at UBC has shown that brief interventions that teach students moderate drinking skills in a group format can reduce frequency of drinking and overall consumption. Marlatt is a leader in developing the concepts behind harm reduction. (p. 399)

10. The first step is detoxification or withdrawal from the drug, often under medical supervision, since effects can be unpleasant and sometimes life-threatening. (p. 397)

11. Residential programs remove addicts from social pressures, support non-use, provide charismatic role models, include confrontive group therapy, and respect addicts as human beings. (p. 402)

12. Research indicates they are of some, but limited, help. They work best when combined with behavioural treatments for psychological factors. (p. 404)

13. A national prevention program in Canada could be implemented for as little as $67 per student, with a net savings over time (due to improved health as a result of decreased smoking) estimated at $619 million per year. (p. 407)

13 Personality Disorders

OVERVIEW

This is the second of three chapters on problems characterized by socially problematic behaviours or traits. Generally, these are not considered "mental illnesses, " as the term is commonly used. However, they do cause considerable unhappiness for affected individuals and/or for those around them.

Chapter 12 covered substance-related problems, including alcohol and drug abuse and dependence. Chapter 13 discusses personality disorders in which people exhibit long-term patterns of thought and behaviour that are ineffective, maladaptive, or socially unacceptable. Examples include social withdrawal, self-centredness, and criminal activity. Chapter 14 deals with problematic sexual behaviours. These include sexual disorders or deviations, such as fetishism and rape, as well as sexual dysfunctions or inadequacies, such as impotence.

Many of the problems in these chapters are characterized by socially disapproved behaviours. Often others want the person to change more than the person him or herself. This raises difficult issues. Can (or should) psychologists change people who do not especially seek change? Are psychologists acting as helpers, as law enforcers, or as moral authorities? Such issues are difficult to answer.

After Chapter 14, the following two chapters cover disorders and issues of childhood (Chapter 15) and old age (Chapter 16). They will complete the text's discussion of psychological disorders. In Chapters 17 and 18, the text turns to general issues in abnormal psychology.

CHAPTER SUMMARY

Personality disorders are long-standing, pervasive, inflexible patterns that impair the individual's functioning in society. *Classifying Personality Disorders: Clusters, Categories, and Problems* presents basic issues in categorizing and applying these labels reliably. Many of these disorders are hard to diagnose reliably and tend to reduce in severity with age more so than treatment.

Assessing personality disorders can pose a difficult problem. Recent research suggests that the focus should be on personality trait dimensions, rather than on personality disorder categories.

In DSM, personality disorders are organized into three clusters. The *Odd/Eccentric Cluster* consists of the paranoid, schizoid, and schizotypal personality disorders. All three have characteristics that seem related to schizophrenia, although research evidence is limited.

The *Dramatic/Erratic Cluster* consists of borderline, histrionic, narcissistic, and anti-social personality disorders. Various theories suggest that all result from forms of distorted and limited parent/child relationships. Anti-social personality disorder is similar to the concept of psychopathy. Research suggests that psychopaths come from families that provided little discipline, love, or effective role models. They experience limited anxiety or empathy in research studies. A contemporary theory hypothesizes a correlation between borderline personality and abuse of one's spouse.

The *Anxious/Fearful Cluster* consists of avoidant, dependent, and obsessive-compulsive personality disorders. Their causes are not widely studied.

Therapies for Personality Disorders have evolved out of clinical practice rather than research knowledge. Borderline personalities present major challenges, and many therapists have adapted therapy approaches for them. Psychological and somatic treatment of psychopaths has been unsuccessful. Prisons remain the common way of handling psychopaths but are used primarily to punish and isolate them.

ESSENTIAL CONCEPTS

1. Personality disorders are characterized by inflexible and pervasive traits that interfere with functioning. These Axis II diagnoses are problematic and dimensional classification may help.

2. Ten personality disorders are defined in *DSM-IV-TR* organized into three clusters.

3. Paranoid, schizoid, and schizotypal personality disorders (the odd/eccentric cluster) have unusual or withdrawn behaviours reminiscent of schizophrenia although research support is limited.

4. Borderline, histrionic, narcissistic, and anti-social personality disorders comprise the dramatic/erratic cluster. Childhood problems have been suspected in these disorders. A contemporary theory hypothesizes a correlation between borderline personality and abuse of one's spouse.

5. Anti-social personality disorder is related to psychopathy, which has been widely studied.

6. Research indicates that psychopaths come from families with anti-social role models, poor discipline, and little love. They experience little anxiety or empathy. In fact, they appear to suppress anxiety.

7. Research by Robert Hare and his students at UBC links psychopaths to brain damage and the under-functioning of various brain centres.

8. Avoidant, dependent, and obsessive-compulsive personality disorders (the anxious/fearful cluster) are not well understood.

9. Therapies for personality disorders have developed out of the experiences of therapists working with them.

10. Borderline personalities present particular challenges for therapists. Many therapists have developed particular therapy approaches for borderlines.

11. Efforts to change anti-social personality disorders have been unsuccessful. Psychotherapeutic and drug approaches have been of limited value. Prisons isolate psychopaths but do little to change their behaviour after release. One school suggests that psychopathy is a related but etiologically different category than anti-social personality disorder.

KEY TERMS

anti-social personality (p. 421)   obsessive-compulsive personality (p. 427)

avoidant personality (p. 426)   paranoid personality (p. 414)

borderline personality (p. 416)   personality disorders (p. 411)

dependent personality (p. 427)   psychopathy (p. 421)

dialectical behaviour therapy (p. 431)   schizoid personality (p. 415)

histrionic personality (p. 419)   schizotypal personality (p. 415)

narcissistic personality (p. 420)

STUDY QUESTIONS

1.   Define personality disorders as a group. How are they different from normal personality styles? (p. 411)

CLASSIFYING PERSONALITY DISORDERS: CLUSTERS, CATEGORIES, AND PROBLEMS (p. 411)

2.   What methods have been investigated in the search for tools to reliably and validly assess personality disorders? Identify the two schools of thought about the basic nature of these disorders. (p. 411)

3. Why are personality disorders placed on Axis II of DSM-IV? Identify two problems in applying these diagnoses, and explain how dimensional classification may help. Identify the three clusters of personality disorders. (p. 412).

ODD/ECCENTRIC CLUSTER (p. 414)

4. Identify and briefly describe the three disorders in the odd/eccentric cluster. What idea has guided the search for causes of these disorders, and how well has this idea proven out so far? (p. 414)

DRAMATIC/ERRATIC CLUSTER (p. 415)

5. For borderline personality disorder, describe the disorder and three views on its etiology. For the next two disorders, describe the disorder and summarize a psychoanalytic view of its etiology. What is the evidence that suggests a link between borderline personality disorder and spouse abuse? (p. 415)

6. Define (and distinguish between) the terms "anti-social personality disorder" and "psychopathy." Summarize data on family background and genetic factors in psychopathy. Why is it desirable to have data on the role of the family that is not retrospective? Describe Hare's concept of the difference between anti-social personality disorder and psychopathy, and describe the nature of the "psychopathy check list" or PCL-R. (p. 421)

7. Regarding emotion and psychopathy, summarize research in three areas indicating little anxiety in psychopaths and in one area indicating little empathy. Also summarize research on response modulation indicating that psychopaths respond impulsively. (p. 421)

ANXIOUS/FEARFUL CLUSTER (p. 426)

8. Briefly describe the three disorders in the anxious/fearful cluster. Give a speculated cause for each of the three disorders. (p. 426)

THERAPIES FOR PERSONALITY DISORDERS (p. 429)

9. How have therapies for personality disorders been developed generally? How have dynamic, behavioural, and cognitive therapists adapted their approaches to work with personality disorders? (p. 429)

10. Why is therapy with borderline personalities especially difficult? Describe two approaches to therapy for borderline personalities, with two or three techniques of each approach. Explain what is meant by saying that the goal of therapy with personality disorders should be to change a "disorder" into a "style. " (p. 430)

11. How effective is psychotherapy with psychopaths and why? Describe the effectiveness of imprisonment in treating psychopaths (two points). Summarize the main findings of the Oak Ridge "G Ward" or Social Therapy Unit. (p. 432)

Self-Test, Chapter 13

(* Items not covered in Study Questions.)

MULTIPLE CHOICE

1. Personality disorders differ from normal personality traits by involving
    a. long-standing and dysfunctional behaviour.
    b. a loss of contact with reality.
    c. personality traits that have become anti-social in nature.
    d. all of the above.

2. A major problem that remains in diagnosing personality disorders is
    a. low reliability over time.
    b. poor inter-rater reliability.
    c. unstructured diagnostic criteria.
    d. very low occurrence in the population for most of the disorders.

3. Which of the following is/are true regarding the assessment of personality disorders?
    a. Researchers use almost exclusively clinical interviews.
    b. The most widely used measure of these disorders is the Millon Clinical Multiaxial Inventory (MCMI).
    c. Recent work suggests that the focus in this area should be put on personality trait dimensions, rather than on disorder categories.
    d. b and c
    e. all of the above

4. The biggest problem with the diagnosis of schizotypal personality disorder is
    a. lack of reliability in making the diagnosis.
    b. difficulty distinguishing it from schizophrenia.
    c. its rarity—it is not clear that the disorder should be listed.
    d. overlap with other personality disorder diagnoses.

5. In object-relations theory, "splitting" refers to the tendency of people with borderline personality disorders to
    a. separate themselves from society.
    b. forget unpleasant events.
    c. see people as all good or all bad.
    d. think illogically.

6. Cleckley emphasized which of the following aspects of anti-social personality that is not emphasized in DSM-IV?
    a. acting out as a child
    b. lack of shame or guilt
    c. recklessness and aggression
    d. impulsive anti-social acts

7. In research on response modulation and psychopathy, psychopaths won or lost money depending on what playing cards appeared. In this research, the impulsivity of psychopaths was studied by
    a. making them wait before deciding to continue the game.
    b. having them estimate the amount of money they had won.
    c. ratings of their verbal statements during the game.
    d. all of the above.

8. Which of the following is not true about the PCL-R of Robert Hare.
    a. It is designed to diagnose personality disorders.
    b. It is a checklist of items that includes callousness and lack of guilt.
    c. It measures two factors, one of which is emotional detachment.
    d. In one study, it successfully predicted treatment outcome in a federal prison.

*9. High rates of which DSM diagnosis have been found in the individuals with dependent personality disorder?

    a.   depression

    b.   schizophrenia

    c.   somatization disorder

    d.   dissociative identity disorder

10. Behaviour and cognitive therapists have generally treated most forms of personality disorder by

    a.   redefining the problem in more behaviour terms.

    b.   doing cognitive therapy that emphasizes that behaviour is state-like and not trait-like.

    c.   using money as a reinforcer to shape socially desirable behaviour.

    d.   working with teachers as a prevention measure for future instances of personality disorders.

11. Dialectical behaviour therapy for patients with borderline personality disorder combines

    a.   social skills training and free-association.

    b.   ego analysis and more directive behavioural techniques.

    c.   behavioural problem-solving and client-centred empathy.

    d.   Gestalt techniques and relaxation training.

12. Psychotherapy with psychopaths is difficult because

    a.   their speech patterns are difficult to understand.

    b.   they are unable to explain reasons for their behaviour.

    c.   therapists are required to report any past misdeeds.

    d.   they do not form open relationships with therapists.

13. The "Oak Ridge experiment" for treating psychopaths is generally considered to be

    a.   an unqualified success.

    b.   a partial success.

    c.   a failure.

    d.   a myth.

SHORT ANSWER

1. Define "personality disorders" (as a group).

2. Why are personality disorders placed on a different axis of *DSM-IV*?

3. Distinguish between schizoid personality and schizotypal personality.

4. Describe Dutton's model of the relationship between borderline personality disorder and spouse abuse.

5. How are histrionic and narcissistic personality disorder the same and different?

6. Research on the role of the family finds that psychopaths tend to come from families characterized by . . .

7. Describe research on response modulation showing impulsivity in psychopaths.

8. Discuss "Factor 1," the most important factor in describing the functioning of psychopaths, as found by the research team headed by Robert Hare of UBC.

9. What is the dimensional approach to the personality disorders?

10. In general, how have therapies for personality disorders been developed?

11. What are the three goals of dialectical behaviour therapy?

12. How effective is the standard treatment for psychopaths?

13. Describe the unique features of the promising "treatment" program for psychopaths developed by Wong and Hare.

ANSWERS TO SELF-TEST, CHAPTER 13

MULTIPLE CHOICE

1. a (p. 411)	2. a (p. 412)	3. d (p. 414)	4. d (p. 415)
5. c (p. 417)	6. b (p. 421)	7. a (p. 421)	8. a (p. 422)
9. a (p. 427)	10. a (p. 431)	11. c (p. 431)	12. d (p. 432)
13. c (p. 434)			

SHORT ANSWER

1. Personality disorders are characterized by enduring, inflexible patterns of inner experience and behaviour that deviate from cultural expectations and cause distress or impairment. (p. 411)

2. This is to remind clinicians to consider their possible presence (in addition to Axis I disorders, which are often the reason the person seeks help). (p. 411)

3. Both have few close friends, but the schizotypal personality also has eccentric ideas, mannerisms, appearance, etc. (p. 415)

4. Dutton suggests that there are three main characteristics of the abusive personality: anger, chronic experience of traumatic symptoms, and borderline personality organization. (p. 417)

5. Both are self-centred. Seemingly, histrionics seek to prove they are special (seek to impress others, etc.), while narcissistics are convinced they already are special (deserve special attention, etc.). (p. 418)

6. rejection, lack of affection, inconsistent discipline, and anti-social fathers. (p. 423)

7. In a card game where the odds of winning decreased steadily, psychopaths continued to play (and lose) longer than normal-, unless required to wait five seconds before deciding whether to continue. (p. 423)

8. Factor 1, referred to as emotional detachment, describes a selfish, remorseless individual with inflated self-esteem who exploits others. This factor focuses on affective and interpersonal characteristics associated with psychopathy. It assesses attributes such as egocentricity, manipulativeness, callousness, and lack of guilt. (p. 422)

9. According to the dimensional approach to personality disorders, these disorders represent extremes of personality traits found in everyone. Most contemporary research focuses on a model of personality called the five-factor model (McCrae & Costa, 1990). The five factors, or major dimensions, of personality are neuroticism, extroversion/ introversion, openness to experience, agreeableness/ antagonism, and conscientiousness. (p. 427)

10. They have been developed by practicing clinicians who report on people they have treated. They have not been based on formal research. (p. 429)

11. The three goals are to help the patients (a) modulate and control their extreme emotionality and behaviours; (b) tolerate feeling distressed; and (c) trust their own thoughts and emotions. (p. 431)

12. The standard treatment (prison) is not very effective at all. In fact, criminologists have argued that prisons are schools for crime. (p. 432)

13. This cognitive-behavioural approach concentrates on "relapse prevention." (p. 435)

Chapter 14

Sexual and Gender Identity Disorders

OVERVIEW

Chapter 14 is the last of three chapters on problems with a social emphasis. Generally, these are not considered "mental illnesses" as such but involve particular behaviours or traits that are of concern to society as well as, sometimes, to the individual. Chapter 12 discussed substance abuse problems that concern both society and the individual to varying degrees. Social and individual concerns about these problems can change dramatically as has happened with cigarette smoking. Chapter 13 discussed personality disorders. Many of these, especially anti-social personality disorders, are clearly more a "problem" for society than for the individual criminal.

Chapter 14 covers sexual problems. Sexual deviations, as the term implies, refer to sexual activities that society considers deviant or aberrant. Like the personality disorders and substance abuse disorders of the last two chapters, defining a sexual activity as "deviant" involves a value judgement. Social and individual concerns can change, as has happened regarding homosexuality. Sexual dysfunctions are common sexual problems involving inhibitions of sexual functioning. Sexual dysfunctions include premature orgasm, vaginismus, and inhibited sexual desire or arousal.

Chapter 14 is the last chapter focusing on socially problematic behaviours. The following two chapters discuss issues and problems of childhood (Chapter 15) and of old age (Chapter 16). Then, the text concludes with two chapters on treatment and legal/ethical issues.

CHAPTER SUMMARY

In *Gender Identity Disorder,* individuals have a sense of themselves as being of one sex although they are anatomically the other sex. Such individuals may seek sex-change surgery to make their physical anatomy consistent with their inner sense of themselves. Behaviour therapy can also help them change their behaviours, sexual fantasies, etc., to match their anatomy.

The *Paraphilias* involve unusual sexual activities or fantasies that the individual either acts on or is markedly disturbed by. They may involve sexual gratification through intimate articles, cross-dressing, or through sexual activities involving pain, children, strangers, etc. Theories of paraphilias often suggest multiple ways they could develop. Behaviour therapists treat such problems using aversion therapy to reduce the unwanted attraction, as well as through social skills training to enable normal sexual relations.

Rape is more an act of violence than of sex. Many professionals view it as a result of social stereotypes. Treatment of rapists is difficult, and attention focuses on helping victims cope with the trauma. Rapists and exhibitionists have a high recidivism rate.

The Sexual Dysfunctions describes dysfunctions as persistent and recurrent inhibitions in sexual functioning that may develop at each stage of the human sexual response cycle. While organic factors may be involved, psychological factors are usually central. Masters and Johnson theorize that historical factors, such as early sexual teachings and experiences, may lead the individual to develop performance fears or adopt a spectator role, thereby inhibiting full participation in sexual activities. Therapies for sexual dysfunctions are highly effective. They focus both on sexual skills and on the relationship.

ESSENTIAL CONCEPTS

1. Gender identity disorders involve feeling that one is the opposite of one's anatomical sex.

2. The two major treatments for gender identity disorders (sex-change surgery and alterations in gender identity) remain controversial.

3. Paraphilias involve a deviation in the object of sexual arousal.

4. The more common paraphilias include fetishism, transvestic fetishism, incest, pedophilia, voyeurism, exhibitionism, sadism, and masochism.

5. Theories of the etiology of paraphilias include fixations at an immature psychosexual stage, accidental classical conditioning, and social skills deficits.

6. Treatment of paraphilias has focused on the behaviour itself via behavioural therapy and judicial interventions. Their effectiveness is unclear and suggests a multi-faceted approach is needed.

7. Rape is often more a crime of aggression and dominance and can have a tremendously adverse impact on the victim. Rapists have a high recidivism rate, and several research programs are looking for treatment protocols that can reduce it.

8. Sexual dysfunctions are inhibitions or disturbances in one of four phases of the human sexual response cycle.

9. The sexual response cycle is described as having appetitive, excitement, orgasm, and resolution phases.

10. Sexual dysfunctions include (in the appetitive phase) hypoactive sexual desire and sexual aversion; (in the excitement phase) female arousal and male erectile disorders; (in the orgasm phase) female or male orgasmic disorders, and premature ejaculation; as well as sexual pain disorders of vaginismus, and dyspareunia.

11. Masters and Johnson proposed that historical factors lead to current factors (performance fears and the spectator role) resulting in sexual dysfunctions.

12. Behavioural and cognitive treatments for sexual dysfunctions are very effective. They include anxiety reduction, education, frank discussion about sexuality, and specific techniques for treating dysfunctions.

KEY TERMS

acquaintance (date) rape (p. 458)

child sexual abuse (p. 451)

dyspareunia (p. 467)

exhibitionism (p. 453)

fear of performance (p. 468)

female orgasmic disorder (p. 466)

female sexual arousal disorder (p. 465)

fetishism (p. 446)

forced rape (p. 458)

frotteurism (p. 454)

gender identity disorder (p. 439)

hypoactive sexual desire disorder (p. 464)

incest (p. 448)

male erectile disorder (p. 465)

male orgasmic disorder (p. 466)

orgasmic reorientation (p. 457)

paraphilias (p. 446)

pedophilia (p. 447)

premature ejaculation (p. 467)

sensate focus (p. 470)

sensory-awareness procedures (p. 470)

sex-reassignment surgery (p. 444)

sexual and gender identity disorders (p. 439)

sexual aversion disorder (p. 464)

sexual dysfunctions (p. 462)

sexual masochism (p. 454)

sexual sadism (p. 454)

sexual value system (p. 470)

spectator role (p. 468)

transvestic fetishism (p. 446)

statutory rape (p. 458)

vaginismus (p. 467)

transsexualism (p. 439)

voyeurism (p. 453)

STUDY QUESTIONS

1. Identify and distinguish among the three kinds of sexual problems discussed in this chapter. (p. 439)

GENDER IDENTITY DISORDERS (p. 439)

2. Define gender identity disorder (GID), noting it is based on inner beliefs. Summarize evidence that hormonal problems and family factors are (and are not) involved. How do cultural values complicate this topic? (p. 439)

3. Describe the steps in treating GID by altering the body. Does this treatment appear effective (and why is its effectiveness difficult to evaluate)? Describe an alternative treatment for altering psychology and its effectiveness. (p. 443)

THE PARAPHILIAS (p. 446)

4. Define paraphilias as a group of disorders. Discuss issues around the terms "recurrent" and "distressed" as opposed to arrest-based definitions. Define seven types of paraphilias and the background or personality factors usually associated with each. (p. 446)

5. Summarize perspectives on the etiology of the paraphilias, including one psychodynamic, four behavioural/ cognitive, and one biological perspective. (p. 446)

6. Describe two general issues in treatment of paraphilias. What has been the impact of psychoanalytic approaches? Describe a range of behavioural and cognitive treatments and their overall effectiveness. Describe biological treatments and issues in their use. (p. 456)

RAPE (p. 458)

7. Is rape considered a sexual crime? Explain. What are the effects of rape on victims during and after the attack? Identify common motivations of rapists. (p. 458)

8. Describe the common approach to treating rapists and its effectiveness. What are the immediate and long-term goals in counselling rape victims? Describe the conflicting findings on treatment programs for rapists from Canadian research. (p. 460)

SEXUAL DYSFUNCTIONS (p. 462)

9. How are sexual dysfunctions different from other sexual problems discussed earlier? Identify four phases of the human sexual response cycle. (p. 462)

10. How common are occasional disturbances in sexual functioning, and when are they labelled dysfunctions? Describe nine sexual dysfunctions organized into four categories. (Note the parallels between these categories and the phases of the human sexual response cycle.) Identify common causes of each dysfunction. (p. 464)

11. According to Masters and Johnson, how do current and historical factors interact to result in sexual dysfunctions? Briefly describe their two current and seven historical factors. (p. 467)

12. Identify five factors suggested by other contemporary views and two general cautions regarding this area. (p. 469)

13. Briefly describe seven techniques used in treating sexual dysfunctions. Notice that, in practice, combinations of these techniques are used. (p. 469)

SELF-TEST, CHAPTER 14

(* Items not covered in Study Questions.)

MULTIPLE CHOICE

1. The sense of being either male or female is referred to as
   a. sexual orientation.
   b. sex-role stereotype.
   c. gender identity.
   d. Oedipal identification.

2. Transsexuals are people who
   a. are attracted to members of the same sex.
   b. dress in the clothing of the opposite sex for sexual gratification.
   c. prefer the company of people of the opposite sex.
   d. identify themselves as members of the opposite sex.

3. Research by Bartlett, Vasey, & Bukowski suggests what about the *DSM-IV-TR* diagnosis of gender identity disorder in children?
   a. It should be divided into separate syndromes for biological males and biological females.
   b. Labelling children with a questionable disorder could stigmatize them.
   c. No distinction is necessary between adult GID and childhood GID, so the syndromes should be combined.
   d. There is insufficient evidence to support it, so it should be dropped from the DSM.
   e. b and c
   f. none of the above

4. A component of psychotherapy prior to sex-reassignment surgery involves
    a. discouraging the patient from seeking surgery, to ensure that they are serious.
    b. focusing on options available that the person may have overlooked, such as removing facial hair or reducing chin size in male-to-female surgery.
    c. training in proper opposite-sex behaviour.
    d. examining underlying causes of opposite gender identity.

5. Recent research has suggested that which of the following does not play a role in the etiology of pedophilia.
    a. lack of empathy
    b. lack of social skills
    c. offender reporting being abused as a child
    d. exposure to child pornography

6. A behavioural hypothesis regarding the etiology of exhibitionism is based on _____ theory.
    a. classical conditioning
    b. operant conditioning
    c. systematic desensitization
    d. modelling

7. Elizabeth is beginning to feel aroused from direct physical contact with her husband. The change in blood flow to her genital area is referred to as
    a. resolution.
    b. tumescence.
    c. appetitive response.
    d. engorgement.

8. Which of the following *DSM-IV-TR* diagnosis has historically been associated with a derogatory label of "frigidity"?
    a. low sex drive
    b. dyspareunia
    c. sexual aversion disorder
    d. female orgasmic disorder

9. Joan experiences pain during sexual intercourse. The frequency of pain has been so frequent that she now dreads the prospect of possible sexual encounters despite experiencing sexual arousal while observing films depicting sexual acts. Joan most likely is suffering from
    a. female orgasmic disorder.
    b. dyspareunia.
    c. imperforate hymen.
    d. major depression.

10. Directed masturbation is often used
    a. to train individuals who have difficulty achieving orgasm.
    b. as a means for redirecting attention from inappropriate sexual stimuli.
    c. for excessive sexual appetite.
    d. as part of a program of treatment for sex offenders.

SHORT ANSWER

1.   How effective is treating gender identity disorder by psychologically changing gender orientation?

2.   Define paraphilias in general.

3.   Define frotteurism.

4.   Describe the relationship between alcohol and sexual offence.

5.   What do most sadists and masochists think and do about their unusual sexual preferences?

6.   How important are biological factors in the paraphilias?

7.   Describe the behavioural approach to treatment of paraphilias.

8.   What are the psychological effects of rape on the victim?

9.   Describe the conclusions of recent research into the previous hypothesis that incest offenders were a low recidivism risk.

10.   Describe the results of Canadian research into the recidivism rates of sexual offenders.

11.   Describe the effectiveness of therapy for rapists.

12.   Summarize other contemporary views of the role of interpersonal factors in sexual dysfunctions.

13.   Compare the typical sexual dysfunction for males with that of females.

14.   List a number of components of therapy for sexual dysfunctions that do not focus directly on sexual activity as such.

ANSWERS TO SELF-TEST, CHAPTER 14

MULTIPLE CHOICE

1. c (p. 439)   2. d (p. 439)   3. e (p. 441)   4. b (p. 444)
5. d (p. 450)   6. a (p. 454)   7. b (p. 464)   8. d (p. 466)
9. b (p. 467)   10. a (p. 470)

SHORT ANSWER

1.   It is difficult to evaluate as most people refuse this approach. Several case studies indicate mixed effectiveness. (p. 443)

2.   Paraphilia refers to attraction to deviant (unusual or unacceptable) sexual activities. The urges must be intense and recurrent so that the individual has acted on them or is markedly distressed by them. (p. 446)

3.   Frotteurism is sexual touching of an unsuspecting person. (p. 454)

4.   Recent Canadian studies suggest that sexual offenders were more likely to be abusers of alcohol than non-sexual violent offenders who still have a high rate of alcohol abuse. (p. 450)

5.   They are relatively comfortable with their preferences and find compatible partners with whom to act out their desires. (p. 454)

6.   Biological factors are not very important. There has been speculation, but research is inconclusive. Biological factors are, at most, only one of many factors. (p. 456)

7.   Procedures are tailored to the individual but often include aversive procedures to decrease inappropriate attractions, positive conditioning of appropriate attractions, and teaching of social skills so the individual can find partners. (p. 456)

8.   Victims feel terrified, vulnerable, and violated during attack. Afterwards, they feel tense, humiliated, angry, or guilty. Nightmares, continued fears, sexual difficulties are common. (p. 459)

9.   Studies in Saskatchewan and Alberta suggest that family-only offenders may still have a low recidivism rate; but incest offenders who also have out-of-family victims have a high risk to re-offend. (p. 460)

10.   Greenberg concludes that rapists and exhibitionist have high levels of recidivism. A recent Canadian study found that men with elevated levels of psychopathy and deviant sexual arousal tended to recidivate sooner and at much higher rates than men low in these factors (Serin, Mailloux, & Malcolm, 2001). (p. 460)

11.   Rapist therapy is difficult to evaluate, but it probably contributes to somewhat lower recidivism. As with paraphilias, treatment is usually attempted in prison with minimally motivated people. (p. 460)

12.   Interpersonal and sexual factors are intertwined. By the time a couple seeks help, one cannot tell whether sex or couple problems started first. (p. 464)

13.   Women diagnosed as having sexual dysfunction tend to lack interest in sex, find it unpleasurable, or fail to achieve orgasm. Men tend to either achieve orgasm too quickly or not at all or have difficulty maintaining an erection. (p. 463)

14.   Options include developing anxiety reduction skills, communication training, and couples therapy focusing on communication issues, etc. (p. 469)

Chapter 15 Disorders of Childhood

OVERVIEW

Chapter 14 concluded three chapters on socially problematic behaviours and traits. This is the first of two chapters devoted to developmental problems and issues. Chapter 15 covers issues and problems that arise in childhood, and Chapter 16 covers issues and problems of old age. Both chapters focus on the general concerns and circumstances of young/old people in our society, as well as on their psychological problems.

Disorders of childhood (this chapter) are complicated by several factors. Children develop and change rapidly. They have difficulty expressing their concerns or asking for help. Not surprisingly, they often receive help for problems that bother the adults around them. Typically these include misbehaviour (hyperactivity and conduct disorders) and educational difficulties (learning disabilities and mental retardation). The chapter also covers childhood autism, a serious and pervasive developmental problem, disorders of overcontrolled behaviour, such as fears and anxiety, and childhood and adolescent depression.

The next chapter, Chapter 16, deals with problems of aging. Older individuals are subject to a wide variety of problems. They must cope with deterioration as well as whatever problems they may have developed over time. More importantly, they must cope with the realization that they are getting older, as well as the fact that society often does not seem to respect, value, or provide for them.

Chapters 15 and 16 complete the text's discussion of specific problems. The last chapters of the text focus on issues related to abnormal psychology. Chapter 17 discusses issues in psychological intervention. Chapter 18 covers legal and ethical issues. Many of these issues have been mentioned throughout the text. The last two chapters provide a more organized and extensive discussion of them.

CHAPTER SUMMARY

Classification of Childhood Disorders is complicated because, as children develop, expectations for their behaviour change.

Disorders of Undercontrolled Behaviour include attention-deficit/hyperactivity disorder and conduct disorder. Children with attention-deficit/hyperactivity disorder have trouble focusing their attention, leading to difficulty in school and play activities. Conduct disorder involves acting-out behaviours, such as juvenile delinquency. Both have been attributed to a wide variety of factors, including biological or genetic deficits and family upbringing.

Learning Disabilities are developmental delays in specific areas (reading, etc.) not related to general intellectual retardation. Research, especially on dyslexia, has suggested problems in specific brain areas. Treatment consists of teaching specific skills. A diagnosis of *Mental Retardation* traditionally involves three criteria: subnormal intellectual functioning, deficits in adaptive behaviour, and onset before age 18. Severe retardation usually results from physical factors, such as chromosomal abnormalities or brain injuries. Mild retardation with no clear cause is much more common and probably results from a combination of biological, motivational, and environmental factors. Social enrichment programs seek to prevent or minimize retardation. Educational and behavioural programs are used to treat problems of retarded individuals as well as improve their intellectual functioning.

Autistic Disorder is, fortunately, an uncommon disorder in which very young children show profound problems in speech, learning, and social relations. Research has not supported early theories which suggested that autistic children had been rejected by emotionally cold parents. Physiological causes have been suggested. Treatment of autism is difficult. Behavioural procedures using modelling and operant conditioning are promising. However, most autistic children remain intellectually and socially limited.

Disorders of Overcontrolled Behaviour include childhood fears and phobias. These disorders in children have characteristics unique to the age of the victim. Separation anxiety and school phobia are manifestations of anxiety that are almost exclusive to children and derive, in part, from the dependence that children have on caregivers and the developmental importance of attachment. For the same reason, treatments for children rely on modelling and family therapy. Added attention is paid to issues of trauma and post-traumatic stress disorder in children in light of the September 11, 2001, terrorist attack in the United States.

There is a growing recognition of the problem of *Depression in Childhood and Adolescence*. It is distressing to observe that major depression and dysthymia occur in children and adolescents as well as in adults. Sometimes depression—often called masked depression—is inferred from behaviours that would not, in adults, be viewed as reflecting an underlying depression (e.g., acting aggressively or misbehaving at school or at home). The etiology of childhood forms of depression focuses on many of the same factors as adult depression, with more emphasis placed on situational factors such as family structure. It is interesting that differences in the rate of affective disorders between the sexes does not occur until adolescence. Prevention of these disorders should be more possible in children because their psychological development is not as established as that of adults.

ESSENTIAL CONCEPTS

1. Disorders of undercontrolled behaviour include hyperactivity and conduct disorders.

2. Attention-deficit/hyperactivity disorder probably has multiple causes and is characterized by inattention, impulsivity, overactivity, academic difficulties, and troubled peer relationships.

3. Conduct disorders tend to be long-lasting difficulties that resist treatment, although newer behavioural and cognitive methods are promising.

4. Learning disabilities are specific developmental problems in an isolated area of academic or daily functioning.

5. Traditional diagnostic criteria for mental retardation are (a) significantly subaverage intellectual functioning, (b) deficits in adaptive behaviour, and (c) onset prior to age 18.

6. There are four classification levels of mental retardation (mild, moderate, severe, and profound), with different IQ scores and prognoses for each level.

7. The specific etiology for most cases of mental retardation is unknown. A combination of biological, motivational, and environmental factors is probably involved. These cases generally fall in the mild category.

8. More severe cases of mental retardation typically result from known physical causes, including Down syndrome, PKU, and various chemical and environmental hazards.

9. Early intervention projects, such as Head Start (Aboriginal Head Start is a similar program in Canada), can minimize or prevent mild mental retardation. Institutional programs and specific behavioural/cognitive programs are also used.

10. Infantile autism is characterized by extreme autistic aloneness, severely limited language, and ritualistic behaviour.

11. The specific etiology of infantile autism remains unknown, although recent work suggests biological, not psychological, factors. Recent advances in understanding the genetic component to the etiology of this disorder have been promising.

12. Highly structured social-learning treatments have been successful in reducing self-injury and in improving communication and self-care skills of autistic children; however, their long-term prognosis is limited.

13. A cluster of childhood disorders, called disorders of overcontrolled behaviour, include anxiety disorders and are caused by traumatic events, including separation and distortions in the development of attachment. Treatments are similar to adult treatments for anxiety, including systematic desensitization and exposure to the feared stimulus while relaxing with adult support.

14. Depression is also considered an overcontrolled behaviour and is linked to loss and to exposure to depressed adults. The symptoms of depression change significantly with age, and differences in the rate of depression found so consistently in the study of adult depression do not develop until adolescence, for reasons not well understood.

KEY TERMS

anxious attachment (p. 516)

conduct disorder (p. 486)

applied behaviour analysis (p. 505)

disorder of written expression (p. 495)

attention-deficit/hyperactivity disorder (p. 479)

disorganized attachment style (p. 516)

autistic disorder (p. 506)

Down syndrome (trisomy 21) (p. 500)

avoidant attachment style (p. 516)

echolalia (p. 508)

expressive language disorder (p. 495)   phonological disorder (p. 495)

fragile X syndrome (p. 501)   profound mental retardation (p. 499)

learning disabilities (p. 495)   pronoun reversal (p. 508)

learning disorders (p. 495)   reading disorder (dyslexia) (p. 495)

masked depression (p. 521)   school phobia (p. 515)

mathematics disorder (p. 495)   secure attachment (p. 516)

mild mental retardation (p. 499)   selective mutism (p. 517)

moderate mental retardation (p. 499)   self-instructional training (p. 505)

motor skills disorder (p. 496)   separation anxiety (p. 515)

oppositional defiant disorder (p. 486)   severe mental retardation (p. 499)

pervasive developmental disorders (p. 506)   social phobia (p. 517)

phenylketonuria (p. 501)   stuttering (p. 495)

STUDY QUESTIONS

CLASSIFICATION OF CHILDHOOD DISORDERS (p. 477)

1.   To classify abnormal behaviour in children, what must diagnosticians consider first and why? (p. 477)

DISORDERS OF UNDERCONTROLLED BEHAVIOUR (p. 479)

2.   What are the characteristics of attention-deficit/hyperactivity disorder (ADHD)? Distinguish between ADHD and "rambunctious kid." Distinguish between ADHD and conduct disorder. (p. 479)

3.   Why is no one theory or factor likely to explain all hyperactivity? Briefly list biological, environmental, and psychological factors that may contribute to hyperactivity. Describe and evaluate two treatments for hyperactivity. (p. 479)

4.   Define conduct disorder and its possible relation to oppositional defiant disorder (ODD). Discuss the prognosis for conduct-disordered children including Moffitt's (1993) proposal. (p. 482)

5.   Identify biological, psychological, and sociological evidence on the etiology of conduct disorder. Describe and evaluate treatment approaches based on incarceration, family intervention, multisystem treatment, anger control, and moral reasoning. (p. 482)

LEARNING DISABILITIES (p. 494)

6.   Define seven learning disabilities in three groups. Briefly identify three possible physiological and three psychological factors in dyslexia. Describe two common approaches to intervention and a common need in any intervention program. (p. 494)

MENTAL RETARDATION (p. 497)

7.   Define "mental retardation" using three traditional criteria. Identify four levels of retardation in *DSM-IV*, including the IQ range and level of social functioning for each. What other approach is encouraged by the American Association of Mental Retardation? (p. 497)

8.   What percentage of retarded individuals have no clearly defined etiology? Identify typical intellectual and social characteristics of these individuals. For those with known etiologies, briefly describe five biological causes with an example of each. (p. 500)

9.   Describe and evaluate five approaches to preventing and/or treating mental retardation. (p. 502)

AUTISTIC DISORDER (p. 506)

10.   What is the distinguishing characteristic of autistic disorder? How do autistic and retarded individuals compare on IQ tests? Describe several characteristics of autism in each of three areas. What is the prognosis for autistic children? (p. 506)

11.   Summarize two early psychological approaches to autism. How well has research supported them? Describe results in two research areas suggesting a biological basis for infantile autism. (p. 510)

12.   List four special problems in treating autistic children. Describe and evaluate three general approaches to treating autism. (p. 512)

DISORDERS OF OVERCONTROLLED BEHAVIOUR (p. 515)

13.   List the types of disorders that are defined as "overcontrolled. " Describe the causes of healthy attachment and the various types of attachment disorders. Discuss the relationship between attachment history and subsequent interpersonal behaviour. (p. 515)

14. Describe treatments for childhood fears and phobias. Discuss the special place of family therapy in the treatment of childhood anxiety. What does the outcome data suggest about the efficacy of treating childhood disorders of overcontrol? Discuss the nature of PTSD in children and its treatment. (p. 517)

DEPRESSION IN CHILDHOOD AND ADOLESCENCE (p. 521)

15. Discuss the prevalence and models of etiology of childhood and adolescent depression. What special problem does "masked depression" pose for children? Discuss the observation that gender differences in rates of depression don't appear until adolescence. Describe the current treatment models and prevention programs for this disorder. (p. 521)

SELF-TEST, CHAPTER 15

(* Items not covered in Study Questions.)

MULTIPLE -CHOICE

*1. The worst prognosis is for those children who have
   a.   only ADHD.
   b.   only conduct disorder.
   c.   both ADHD and conduct disorder.
   d.   all of the above have equally poor prognoses.

2. The genetic factors that are inherited by children with ADHD are
   a.   brain function and structure.
   b.   neurotransmitter function and specificity.
   c.   appetitive and metabolic functions.
   d.   all of the above.

3. Which of the following is not a symptom of oppositional defiant disorder?
   a.   stealing
   b.   temper tantrums
   c.   refusing to follow directions
   d.   annoying others deliberately

4. According to Dodge and Frame (1982), aggressive children demonstrate cognitive biases in situations
   a.   in which peers act aggressively.
   b.   in which peers act in a prosocial manner.

    c.   which are ambiguous.

    d.   in which they are rejected.

5.   Which of the following is not a change brought in by the new Canadian Youth Criminal Justice Act?

    a.   It promotes alternatives to court for nonviolent crimes.

    b.   It lowers the age from 16 to 14 for possible adult sentences for serious crimes.

    c.   It creates a repeat offenders category for youth.

    d.   It gives victims a greater role in sentencing.

    e.   All of the above.

    f.   None of the above.

*6.   Henggeler's work involves studying programs for delivering intensive and comprehensive therapy services in the community, targeting the adolescent, the family, the school, and in some cases the peer group. This type of delivery is called _____ therapy.

    a.   comprehensive

    b.   multisystematic

    c.   psychodynamic

    d.   cognitive behavioural

7.   The *DSM-IV* diagnosis of mental retardation requires both low intellectual functioning and

    a.   poor social skills.

    b.   poor adaptive skills.

    c.   poor academic achievement.

    d.   inability to hold a job.

8.   Mildly retarded adults

    a.   are about twice as likely to be institutionalized as nonretarded individuals.

    b.   usually have learning disabilities that prevent them from attending school beyond the 6th grade.

    c.   have usually learned academic skills up to about the 10th grade level but rarely have graduated from high school.

    d.   can usually work at unskilled jobs and help support themselves financially.

*9.   The "bump" in the normal curve showing the theoretical distribution of IQ scores

    a.   represents the number of expected cases of mentally retarded individuals in the population.

    b.   is a misnomer, because there is actually an extreme flattening in the curve.

    c.   is the area where there is a higher than expected number of cases of mentally retarded individuals.

    d.   has not been observed in epidemiology estimates.

*10.   Autism was formerly considered a form of

    a.   learning disability.

    b.   mental retardation.

    c.   schizophrenia.

    d.   conduct disorder.

*11 A major difference between autism and Asperger's syndrome is that
   a.   children with autism are more active than those with Asperger's.
   b.   children with Asperger's usually have better language development.
   c.   children with autism are usually more attached.
   d.   none of the above.

12. Early theorists emphasized the role of _____ in the etiology of autism.
   a.   exposure to war or other traumas
   b.   biological factors
   c.   bad parenting
   d.   well-meaning but overindulgent parents

13. Which of the following is not one of the attachment styles described by Ainsworth?
   a.   securely attached
   b.   anxiously attached
   c.   aggressively attached
   d.   avoidant attachment

14. Which of the following is the main symptom of PTSD in children that differentiates it from adult symptomotology?
   a.   generalized nightmares
   b.   repetitive play
   c   omen information, a belief in their ability to predict the future
   d.   all of the above
   e.   none of the above

15. Which best describes the experience of drug therapy in treating childhood depression?
   a.   Drug therapies do not seem to be very effective with children.
   b.   Drug therapy is about as effective with children as adults.
   c.   Drug therapy helps a higher percentage of children who try it than adults.
   d.   Drug therapy is not used for children.

SHORT ANSWER

1.   What issue must be considered before diagnosing any childhood disorder?

2.   Distinguish between ADHD and "rambunctious kid."

3.   How effective are drug treatments for hyperactivity?

4.   Describe what is done in family intervention with conduct-disordered children.

5. Compare the boot camp approach used in Project Turnaround in Ontario to the program developed at the Response Program of the Maples Adolescent Centre in British Columbia.

6. Summarize the evidence regarding visual perceptual deficits as a basis for dyslexia.

7. Describe PKU as a cause of mental retardation.

8. Describe the activities of two Canadian provinces in the North American eugenics movement.

9. Describe the effectiveness of the Head Start project as a means of preventing mental retardation.

10. Describe common communication deficits of autistic children.

11. What research suggests a genetic basis for autism?

12. Summarize research on drug treatments for autism.

13. Describe the research findings suggesting a link between avoidant attachment style and interpersonal style.

14. Describe the major symptoms of separation anxiety.

ANSWERS TO SELF-TEST, CHAPTER 15

MULTIPLE CHOICE

1. c (p. 482)	2. a (p. 483)	3. a (p. 486)	4. c (p. 490)	5. e (p. 491)
6. b (p. 492)	7. d (p. 495)	8. c (p. 499)	9. c (p. 500)	10. c (p. 506)
11. b (p. 506)	12. c (p.510)	13. d (p. 516)	14. a (p. 519)	15. a (p. 523)

SHORT ANSWER

1. One has to consider what behaviour is normal for the age, because the "symptoms" may be typical. (p. 477)

2. Many kids are active and rambunctious. ADHD is for extreme and persistent problems, not just kids who are more active than parents or teachers prefer. (p. 481)

3. Drugs improve concentration and reduce behaviour problems but have little effect on long-term academic achievement and have side effects. (p. 484)

4. Parental behaviour management training emphasizing positive reinforcement of prosocial behaviour plus time-outs, age-appropriate consequences, etc. (p. 490)

5. "Project Turnaround" is run by the private sector in a jail converted for the purpose. The military milieu provides a structure where attention is focused on positive activities and progress is rewarded by "promotion." The guiding premise of the Maples program is that an insecure attachment style is at the root of the conduct disorder. Interventions include family therapy and parent training, as well as individually focused treatment. (p. 493)

6. Research has not supported past theories linking dyslexia to perceptual deficits, such as seeing letters backwards. (p. 495)

7. PKU is a genetic inability to process phenylalanine, a protein amino acid. Without a special diet, phenylalanine accumulates in the body, producing brain damage and retardation. (p. 501)

8. Alberta and British Columbia passed laws in the 1920s and 1930s that legalized involuntary sterilization for those labelled "mentally defective." In Alberta alone, 2,102 people identified as "mental defectives" and 370 psychotics were sterilized before the laws were rescinded in 1972. (p. 503)

9. Research shows that children in Head Start programs improve on several social and academic measures but remain behind their peers. (p. 504)

10. Half never speak at all. Others have speech peculiarities including echolalia, pronoun reversal, and neologisms. (p. 506)

11. The risk of autism rises dramatically in siblings of autistics, up to 91 percent in identical twins of autistics. (Family studies are not possible since autistics rarely marry.) (p. 510)

12. Several drugs have been tried with mixed success. They produce some improvement in some autistic children but have side effects. (p. 513)

13. Attachment style is also associated with maladaptive interpersonal styles. A study conducted by Canadian researchers yielded evidence indicating that male adolescents with an avoidant attachment style are more likely than those with a secure attachment style to express and receive coercive behaviours in dating relationships. (p. 516)

14. Separation anxiety involves an unrealistic concern about separation from major attachment figures, with the levels of anxiety being above the level associated typically with the child's developmental level. These symptoms include unrealistic and persistent worries about harm to major attachment figures, along with fears of abandonment, refusal to go to school due to a need to stay close to an attachment figure, an avoidance of being alone, the experience of nightmares involving separation themes, and the experience of physical complaints in anticipation of being separated from attachment figure. (p. 515)

Chapter 16 Aging and Psychological Disorders

OVERVIEW

Chapter 16 is the concluding chapter on developmental problems. Chapter 15 discussed disorders of childhood and growing up. Chapter 16 is devoted to the problems of aging and growing old. Both young and old people in our society are vulnerable. Others do not always think about their special circumstances and needs or provide the care and attention they may need. This is more true for older than for younger people—a disturbing thought for those who plan to live long enough to grow old.

Chapter 16 completes the text's discussion of specific psychological disorders. The last two chapters of the text deal more intensively with issues in abnormal psychology. Chapter 17 evaluates various treatment methods and discusses issues in integrating them. Finally, Chapter 18 covers legal and ethical issues. Legal issues include issues regarding the insanity defence and commitment of disturbed individuals. Ethical issues cover rights of therapy clients and research participants. Earlier chapters have mentioned these topics in various contexts. The last two chapters bring together and complete these discussions.

CHAPTER SUMMARY

Growing old is obviously a time of physical decline. Medical problems become an increasing concern. Beyond the purely medical aspects of old age, however, are a wide range of psychological and social problems.

The chapter begins by summarizing *Issues, Concepts, and Methods in the Study of Older Adults*. This discussion forms a basis for considering physical and psychological disorders of older adults.

Old Age and Brain Disorders covers two disorders. Dementias are slow developing, progressive conditions that are usually irreversible and require supportive care. Deliriums develop suddenly and, if recognized, can often be reversed by treating the underlying physical conditions.

Old Age and Psychological Disorders emphasizes factors that make the elderly more (or less) susceptible to various problems. Depression often accompanies physical and psychological declines as people grow old. Anxiety problems may continue from younger years or develop as new issues emerge. Suspiciousness and paranoia may result as the elderly have difficulty understanding others due to hearing problems and social isolation. The elderly are also subject to other psychological problems. Suicide may result as they struggle to accept changing physical and social situations. Contrary to popular conceptions, older adults are capable of enjoying and engaging in sexual activity despite slowed biological responses.

Treatment and Care of Older Adults is complicated by stereotypes and misinformation among professionals. Nursing homes and other facilities often fail to encourage the elderly to maintain their skills and capabilities. Community-based services could help the elderly remain as independent as possible. *Issues Specific to Therapy with Older Adults* include changing social and personal realities. Therapists can adjust the content and process of therapy to reflect these issues. The problems related to the abuse of the elderly and the status of home care in Canada are discussed.

Issues Specific to Therapy with Older Patients results from recognition of the unique needs and associated disorders of the elderly. Geriatric teams and multi-dimensional preventative programs developed in Canada have shown promise in the prevention or amelioration of disorders associated with aging.

ESSENTIAL CONCEPTS

1.   Age effects, cohort effects, and time-of-measurement effects complicate research efforts to understand older adults.

2.   Dementia is a gradual deterioration of intellectual abilities over several years, until functioning becomes impaired. It is estimated that the prevalence of Alzheimer's disease will quadruple and that 106 million people worldwide will have the disease by 2050. While there are environmental factors in the cause of Alzheimer's disease it has a very high heritability rate of 76 percent.

3.   Many cases of dementia are irreversible. Treatment consists of support and assistance in living as independently as possible.

4.   Most dementia patients are in the care of their families, and support for these families is valuable, especially when they must decide about institutionalization.

5.   Delirium is a clouded state of consciousness characterized by difficulty concentrating and maintaining a directed stream of thought. Many cases of delirium are reversible if detected in time.

6.   There is a tendency to attribute the behaviour of older adults to the fact that they are older. This can lead to erroneous conclusions about the effects of aging and cause practitioners to overlook the individual's uniqueness.

7.   Difficulties of growing old can contribute to psychological problems, including depression, paranoid disorder, abuse of prescription drugs, and insomnia. A recent survey of 2,341 elderly Canadians found that 2.6 percent had major depression (5 or more symptoms) and 4.9 percent had minor depression (2 to 4 symptoms).

8.   Aging individuals have unique patterns of sleep disorders, in that they tend to have difficulty staying asleep rather than falling asleep. Cognitive treatments appear to be more effective than drug treatments for these individuals.

9.   Most older adults maintain sexual interest and engage in sexual activity, although there may be a general slowing of the sexual response cycle, and the intensity of sexual arousal may not be as great.

10.   Regardless whether they are cared for in the community or in a nursing home, giving the aged responsibility for self-care, planning, and control over their lives is important to their continued psychological and physical well-being.

11.   Psychotherapy with the elderly requires sensitivity to their special issues. The elderly can benefit from help in coping with the realistic problems of old age.

12.   As with psychological disorders of any age, prevention is more effective than treatment. A multidisciplinary approach to the prevention of mental disorders in the elderly is particularly important.

KEY TERMS

age effects (p. 530)   longitudinal studies (p. 531)

ageism (p. 529)   neurofibrillary tangles (p. 533)

Alzheimer's disease (p. 533)   paraphrenia (p. 546)

cognitive reserve hypothesis (p. 535)   plaques (p. 533)

cohort effects (p. 530)   selective mortality (p. 531)

cross-sectional studies (p. 531)   sleep apnea (p. 549)

delirium (p. 539)   time-of-measurement effects (p. 531)

dementia (p. 532)

STUDY QUESTIONS

ISSUES, CONCEPTS, AND METHODS IN THE STUDY OF OLDER ADULTS (p. 530)

1.   How does diversity change in groups of older people? Identify three effects that complicate research on aging. Include a description of factors that complicate both cross-sectional and longitudinal studies. Describe two other factors that make it difficult to know about psychological problems in older adults. Describe the demographic changes that are making aging a critical issue in Canada. (p. 530)

OLD AGE AND BRAIN DISORDERS (p. 532)

2.   Define two forms of brain disorder that can affect the elderly (p. 532). Describe common symptoms and the common cause of dementia in older adults. What are the physiological changes and genetic factors in Alzheimer's? What are the goals of treatment from biological and psychosocial perspectives? (p. 533)

3.   Describe common symptoms of delirium and distinguish them from symptoms of dementia. What are common causes and treatment? (p. 539) Describe the most important findings of the Nun study of the progression of Alzheimer's disease. (p. 536)

OLD AGE AND PSYCHOLOGICAL DISORDERS (p. 540)

4.   How common are psychological problems among the elderly? (p. 540) List the eight psychological problems covered in this section. (p. 541)

5.   The text describes depression, anxiety, and delusional (paranoid) disorders. For each problem describe (a) how it differs in older people, (b) possible causes, and (c) treatment. (p. 541)

6.   Briefly describe two or three issues for each of the following topics (a) schizophrenia, (b) alcohol abuse, (c) abuse of illegal drugs, and (d) medication misuse in older adults. (p. 546)

7.   Describe the causes and treatment of three other psychological problems among the elderly. (p. 548)

8.   Describe the findings of Morin et al regarding the nature of sleeping disorders of the elderly and their treatment. (p. 550)

TREATMENT AND CARE OF THE ELDERLY (p. 553)

9.   Identify three general issues in treatment and care of the elderly. (p. 553)

10.   What is a common effect on family caregivers of nursing home placement? Summarize a study suggesting subtle problems in nursing home care and possible reasons for the results. Identify two other reasons for poor physical and mental health care. Describe community-based care and three problems in caring for the elderly in the community. (p. 554)

11.   What is the current state of home care services for the elderly in Canada? Describe the extent of and the types of abuse of the elderly presented in the textbook. Discuss methods of preventing this type of abuse. (p. 554)

ISSUES SPECIFIC TO THERAPY WITH OLDER ADULTS (p. 559)

12.   Identify six content and five process issues in providing therapy to older adults. (p. 560)

SELF-TEST, CHAPTER 16

(* Items not covered in Study Questions.)

MULTIPLE CHOICE

*1.   Setting the age at which one is considered "old," which is now 65, is based on
   a.   clear biological changes that begin at about that age.
   b.   social policy.
   c.   the age at which individuals begin to refer to themselves as old.
   d.   a scientific standard.

2.   Disorders of old age in *DSM-IV*
      a.   have been revised substantially from the previous DSMs.
      b.   are basically the same as those of younger adults.
      c.   are included in a separate section for the first time.
      d.   are basically similar to Axis II disorders.

3.   Plaques, which develop as part of Alzheimer's disease, are
      a.   fatty deposits in areas of the brain.
      b.   cholesterol remains from poor diet.
      c.   remnants of lost neurons and a waxy protein.
      d.   equivalent to neurofibrillary tangles.

4.   Which of the following is not a confirmed risk factor for Alzheimer's disease?
      a.   a family history of Alzheimer's disease
      b.   breaks in the DNA of chromosome 12
      c.   head trauma
      d.   lower education
      e.   none of the above

5.   Delirium can occur only
      a.   after age 70.
      b.   following a stroke.
      c.   after a significant life stressor such as loss of a spouse.
      d.   None of these are correct. Delirium can occur at any time.

6.   Depression in older adults can be distinguished from depression in younger adults by higher levels of
      a.   somatic complaints.
      b.   suicidal ideation.
      c.   hostility.
      d.   agitation.

7.   Paraphrenia differs from schizophrenia in that paraphrenia is associated with
      a.   more negative symptoms.
      b.   more hallucinations and paranoia.
      c.   reduced Parkinson's from antipsychotic medications.
      d.   fewer social skills deficits.

8.   Epidemiologists forecast that in the years to come
      a.   cannabis and heroin use will decline among older adults.
      b.   fewer older adults will enter methadone treatment clinics.
      c.   there will be a sharp rise in cocaine use among older adults.
      d.   cannabis use will increase among older adults.

9.   A recent Canadian study concludes that the abuse of which drug is more prevalent in older people than previously thought?
    a.   alcohol
    b.   prescription drugs
    c.   nicotine
    d.   marijuana

10. A side effect of sleep drugs, especially among older adults, is
    a.   reduced REM sleep.
    b.   insomnia.
    c.   respiratory difficulties.
    d.   all of the above.

11. Morin found that the type of sleeping disorder experienced by the elderly tends to be
    a.   sleep walking.
    b.   difficulty getting to sleep.
    c.   difficulty staying asleep.
    d.   sleep apnea.

12. Which of the following is a recommended content issue in therapy with older adults?
    a.   Encouraging clients to make new social contacts.
    b.   Helping clients deal directly with fear of death.
    c.   Not attributing personal problems to medical or social problems.
    d.   Keeping up spirits despite difficulties.

13. Which of the following is not a type of elder abuse identified in the text?
    a.   financial abuse through misappropriation of funds by family or caregivers
    b.   neglect including malnourishment and dehydration
    c.   psychological or emotional abuse
    d.   sexual abuse
    e.   all of the above
    f.   none of the above

SHORT ANSWER

1.   Are older people more similar to or more different from younger people? Explain briefly.

2.   Your older friend seems confused. What behaviours might you look for to determine if your friend is experiencing delirium or dementia?

3.   Describe the basic methodology and goal of the Nun study.

4.   Why do we tend to ignore psychological problems in older people?

5.   Briefly describe the technique of reminiscence therapy.

6.   What are common causes of paranoia in the elderly?

7.   Briefly describe the issues in medication misuse among the elderly.

8.   Identify three general issues in treatment and care of the elderly.

9.   Summarize a study suggesting that even good quality care in a nursing home may be undesirable.

10.   Briefly describe the main cause for the lower level of care in nursing homes in the United States vs. that in Canada.

11.   Identify three problems in caring for the elderly in the community.

12.   Explain "life review" as an issue in therapy with the elderly.

13.   Describe the main features of the PRISMA project that have likely led to positive results.

ANSWERS TO SELF-TEST, CHAPTER 16

MULTIPLE CHOICE

1. b (p. 539)   2. b (p. 531)   3. c (p. 553)   4. b (p. 533)
5. d (p. 539)   6. a (p. 541)   7. b (p. 546)   8. d (p. 547)
9. a (p. 547)   10. d (p. 549)   11. c (p. 550)   12. b (p. 561)
13. e (p. 556)

SHORT ANSWER

1. Despite stereotypes, older people are more diverse than younger. (p. 529)

2. Delirium tends to have rapid onset, with not just forgetful but also overtly confused thinking and speech. The person with delirium might be more acutely bewildered, his or her sleep-wake cycles more disrupted, and nightmares and hallucinations more likely than with dementia. An individual with dementia will likely show a gradual onset, faulty orientation with time and place, and be confused about everyday events and routines. (p. 532)

3. The goal of the Nun study is to unlock the secrets of the cause and progress of Alzheimer's disease. A group of 678 Catholic nuns are allowing researchers to look at their personal and medical records, to undergo cognitive testing on an annual basis, and to autopsy their brains at death. (p. 536)

4. We assume problems are due to old age and physical decline. This is not true or is only partly true in most cases. (p. 540)

5. Reminiscence or life review therapy asks individuals to reflect on previous negative events and address any remaining conflict as well as strive to find meaning in one's present life. (p. 543)

6. Paranoia results from attempts to fill in gaps in understanding caused by memory or sensory losses, social isolation, etc. (p. 545)

7. Illnesses result in using more drugs, while changing metabolism increases risk of side effects. Multiple drugs may interact. Elderly may get confused and take drugs incorrectly. Limited finances lead the elderly to not take drugs as prescribed and to share drugs. (p. 548)

8. Professionals are less likely to notice and refer problems. They have lower expectations for improvement—despite the elderly being more thoughtful and thus, seemingly, more amenable to therapy. (p. 553)

9. Elderly people were randomly assigned to three intensities of professional care. Results showed that more professional involvement increased death rates because the professionals pushed for institutional placement. (p. 555)

10. The situation with regard to care for the elderly is much worse in the United States than Canada due to the lower training and pay levels for nursing assistants. (p. 554)

11. (a) Coordinating services among many agencies with various rules can be difficult. (b) Health care professionals often don't enjoy working with the problems of the elderly. (c) There can be conflicts with family members who feel angry, guilty, etc. over care issues. (p. 555)

12. Older people often seek and may benefit from reviewing their lives and considering the meaning and implications of their lives and experiences. (p. 560)

13. The PRISMA project uses recent advances in assessment tools, a high degree of planning and coordination across disciplines, and high staff/client ratios. (p. 561)

17 Outcomes and Issues in Psychological Intervention

OVERVIEW

The previous chapter completed the text's discussion of major forms of abnormal behaviour. Chapter 17 begins the last section of the text, which covers issues in abnormal psychology. These issues underlie many topics covered earlier and round out discussion of the field.

Chapter 17 discusses issues in psychological intervention. Psychological interventions for various disorders were covered in the chapters on those disorders. Chapter 17 brings these interventions together and discusses efforts to integrate them. Chapter 18 deals with legal and ethical issues. Legal issues include insanity, competency to stand trial, and involuntary commitment. Ethical issues concern the rights of research participants and therapy clients.

CHAPTER SUMMARY

Chapter 17 is devoted to evaluating, comparing, and integrating psychological interventions. Many of these approaches to psychological treatment were introduced in earlier chapters.

General Issues in Evaluating Psychotherapy Research discusses the related but different goals of psychotherapy researchers seeking to conduct quality research and psychotherapists seeking to help individuals in the real world.

Review of Psychoanalytic Therapies summarizes therapy approaches growing out of Freud's work. Classical psychoanalysis focuses on repressed childhood conflicts, while briefer analytic approaches focus more on current life issues. These approaches have been evaluated based on theoretical issues and research on their effectiveness.

Review of Client-Centred Therapy covers Carl Rogers' approach. Rogers's originated the field of psychotherapy research, and his model has shown modest effectiveness. *Review of Gestalt Therapy* discusses the similar but more technique-oriented Gestalt approach which has been less studied.

Review of Behavioural and Cognitive Therapies reviews and evaluates counterconditioning, operant, and cognitive therapies. Growing out of research traditions, these approaches have been more clearly defined and studied in recent years. For example, Ellis' and Beck's cognitive approaches have been extensively studied and compared. Other issues in this area include questions of how to generalize and maintain therapy gains. Generally, these approaches have shown considerable effectiveness and raise significant issues for the field.

Review of Couples and Family Therapy and *Review of Community Psychology* explains couple, family, and community approaches to intervention and issues in their use.

Psychotherapy Integration discusses efforts to bring together the various approaches. Wachtel's classic effort to integrate psychoanalysis and behaviour therapy illustrates how seemingly disparate approaches to therapy can benefit from each other's ideas. More generally, Lazarus and Messer have debated ways of integrating therapy approaches and the desirability of doing so. Meichenbaum's constructivist cognitive-behavioural treatment model is a recent attempt at integration.

ESSENTIAL CONCEPTS

1. Psychological interventions can be evaluated in terms of both their theoretical assumptions and their empirical effectiveness.

2. Research is essential to evaluate and improve psychotherapy. However, research's need for standardization differs from therapists' need to individualize therapy for each client.

3. Even though therapists tend to identify with one school of psychotherapy, when asked about the general nature of the process, they tend to agree across schools and methods.

4. Classic psychoanalysis (which seeks to lift childhood repressions) and briefer psychodynamic therapies (focusing more on current life issues) are difficult to evaluate. The nature of "insight" and "therapeutic relationship" raises important, complex issues. Generally, research shows inconsistent to modest benefits.

5. Client-centred therapy assumes that by valuing clients and understanding their perspective, therapists can create conditions in which clients can find their own answers and goals. Psychotherapy research originated in client-centred therapy and has shown general benefits, although core assumptions of the theory remain unclear.

6. Gestalt therapists have developed many powerful techniques but resist formal evaluation of their effectiveness.

7. Behavioural and cognitive approaches have led to a wide range of therapy techniques.

8. Counterconditioning techniques (based on classical conditioning) have proven effective with a wide range of problems. Operant techniques have also been effective, especially with children.

9. Cognitive therapists propose that actions (and problems) result from the way people make sense out of their world. Cognitive therapists include Ellis and Beck.

10. Ellis seeks to convince clients that their irrational assumptions lead to difficulties. Research supports his approach in some cases, although deciding what assumptions are "irrational" becomes ethically complex. Beck encourages people to examine the evidence for their assumptions and has had success, although the way in which his methods lead to change is unclear.

11. Cognitive and behavioural therapies have paid special attention to how therapy progress can be generalized and maintained after therapy ends.

12. Cognitive and behavioural therapies are more subtle than is initially obvious. They address many historical issues in psychology and, in practice, utilize a range of approaches to effect change.

13. Couples and family therapists use a wide range of approaches to address communication problems that develop in long-term relationships. They have shown significant results although pragmatic issues remain.

14. Integration of various interventions remains a challenge. Wachtel has proposed integrating psychoanalysis and behavioural therapies. He emphasizes that current behaviours may both reflect and maintain childhood issues in a cyclical manner and that each theory can benefit from the methods and emphases of the other.

15. Integration of psychotherapy schools can occur in many ways, as Lazarus and Messer showed through a debate. Lazarus argued for adopting useful techniques from any theory without adopting the theory. Messer argued that we can only understand and utilize techniques in terms of theories. Although Meichenbaum's approach is applicable to a wide array of problems, constructivism has made its most significant contributions to Dobson and Pusch's depth dimension.

16. Community psychology seeks to prevent problems in populations. Doing so is a challenge and is difficult to evaluate. This approach grew out of and continues to reflect the social activism issues of the 1960s.

KEY TERMS

common factorism (p. 592)

mental health promotion (p. 594)

community psychology (p. 593)

stepped care (p. 569)

Dodo bird effect (p. 568)

technical eclecticism (p. 591)

effectiveness (p. 567)

theoretical integration (p. 592)

efficacy (p. 567)

therapeutic (working) alliance (p. 573)

empirically informed therapies (p. 570)

triadic reciprocality (p. 582)

empirically supported therapies (ESTs) (p.570)

STUDY QUESTIONS

GENERAL ISSUES IN EVALUATING PSYCHOTHERAPY RESEARCH (p. 565)

1. Describe four differences between therapy as researched and therapy as practiced and the basis or reason for each. Describe two impacts of managed care and two ways some professionals are responding to it. (p. 565)

REVIEW OF PSYCHOANALYTIC THERAPIES (p. 571)

2. Describe three basic emphases in classical psychoanalysis and four modifications of it. (p. 571)

3. Briefly identify five general issues in the evaluation of classical psychoanalysis. Describe four conclusions of research on classical psychoanalysis. Evaluate brief psychodynamic therapies by summarizing the result of outcome research and four results of process research. (p. 572)

REVIEW OF CLIENT-CENTRED THERAPY (p. 575)

4. Summarize the basic concepts of client-centred therapy in about five points. Evaluate client-centred therapy in eight points. (p. 575)

REVIEW OF GESTALT THERAPY (p. 577)

5. Why has little research been done on Gestalt therapy? Summarize the basic concepts of Gestalt therapy in three points and evaluate it in two points. (p. 577)

REVIEW OF BEHAVIOURAL AND COGNITIVE THERAPIES (p. 578)

6.   In general, how do behavioural and cognitive methods approach therapy? Evaluate counterconditioning and exposure methods by describing their approach to therapy and their effectiveness (two points each). Evaluate operant methods by describing their approach to therapy and their effectiveness (two points each). (p. 578)

7.   For Ellis' cognitive (rational-emotive) approach describe (a) its goal, (b) its general effectiveness, and (c) why defining irrationality involves an issue of ethics. For Beck's cognitive approach describe (a) its goal in comparison to Ellis, (b) its general effectiveness, and (c) two other issues. Compare these two approaches in three points. Summarize six additional reflections on cognitive behaviour therapy. (p. 579)

8.   What is meant by "generalization and maintenance of treatment effects?" Identify five ways cognitive and behavioural therapists encourage these goals. Summarize the text's views of five basic issues in cognitive and behaviour therapy. (p. 579)

REVIEW OF COUPLES AND FAMILY THERAPY (p. 585)

9.   What concept underlies all couples and family therapies? Evaluate these approaches by describing (a) their general effectiveness and (b) predictors of good and poor outcomes. (p. 585)

PSYCHOTHERAPY INTEGRATION (p. 590)

10.   Summarize Wachtel's view on integrating psychoanalysis and behaviour therapy by describing (a) his principal position and (b) four things behaviour therapists can learn from psychoanalysts. (p. 590)

11.   Identify three general ways in which psychotherapy approaches can be integrated. Summarize Lazarus' views on the topic in three points. Also discuss Meichenbaum's "constructivist" model. Why does the text argue against premature integration? (p. 592)

REVIEW OF COMMUNITY PSYCHOLOGY (p. 593)

12. What is the basic goal of community psychology? Evaluate this area by identifying three reasons it is difficult to study. Summarize two political factors that contributed to the development of community psychology and two issues in the field currently. (p. 593)

SELF-TEST, CHAPTER 17

(* Items not covered in Study Questions.)

MULTIPLE CHOICE

1. Most therapists describe themselves as
   a. behavioural.
   b. cognitive-behavioural.
   c. dynamic.
   d. eclectic.

2. Which of the following are considered to be "harmful" therapies by the text?
   a. critical incident stress debriefing
   b. boot-camp interventions
   c. DID-oriented therapies
   d. all of the above
   e. none of the above

3. The advent of managed care has changed what aspect of practice for psychologists?
   a. theoretical orientation
   b. focus upon underlying causes
   c. accountability
   d. efficacy

4. When asked about the general nature of psychotherapy, therapists from across a wide spectrum of schools tend to
   a. disagree as to the general nature and purposes of psychotherapy.
   b. agree as to the general nature and purposes of psychotherapy.
   c. agree as to the procedures, but disagree as to the general goals.
   d. refuse to answer questions of this nature.

5. Which of the following is not allowed in the Canadian health care system?
   a. private hospitals
   b. managed care
   c. fee for service health care
   d. user fees

6.   Early in therapy, Tom has found that he enjoys meeting with his therapist. The two seem to be working toward a common goal, and the time appears to go quickly. This would characterize a good
    a.   efficacy.
    b.   initial symptom reduction.
    c.   process.
    d.   working alliance.

7.   Exposure and counterconditioning methods have been most effective in treating
    a.   anxiety.
    b.   children.
    c.   addictions.
    d.   criminals.

8.   A common element across therapies, regardless of paradigm, is
    a.   focusing directly upon symptoms.
    b.   challenging irrational beliefs.
    c.   determining stimuli that control dysfunctional behaviour.
    d.   maintaining a positive relationship between therapist and client.

9.   According to Lazarus, one problem in rapprochement between different theories of psychotherapy
    a.   is that adherents to different theories simply cannot process the necessary information across all paradigms.
    b.   is based in large part on empirical findings.
    c.   has been based in reluctance to find common factors.
    d.   is based on how different approaches define facts.

10.   Which of the following are factors that contribute to better outcome in therapy?
    a.   similarity of cultural background between client and therapist
    b.   same gender for therapist and client
    c.   similarity of ethnic background
    d.   all of the above

11.   Which of the following is true of the Alberta "telemental health service"?
    a.   It offers the services of telepathic health care providers.
    b.   It receives very high satisfaction ratings.
    c.   It is not acceptable to most rural Albertans who need mental health services.
    d.   It is acceptable to most residents but is too expensive compared to traditional services.

12.   The basic goal of community psychology is
    a.   affordable treatment.
    b.   community-based treatment.
    c.   stable communities.
    d.   prevention.

SHORT ANSWER

1. Discuss the findings of Boisvert and Faust (2003) about what experts believe about the general nature of psychotherapy, regardless of school.

2. Describe the theoretical view of ego analysts.

3. According to Carl Rogers' client-centred therapy, what are the characteristics of healthy people?

4. What does the text conclude about the therapist qualities emphasized by Rogers?

5. Describe the procedure of motivational interviewing.

6. In general, how do behavioural and cognitive methods approach therapy?

7. Describe the basic model behind emotion-focused couples therapy.

8. What concept underlies all couples and family therapies?

9. Summarize the principal position on psychoanalysis and behaviour therapy.

10. Why does the text argue against premature integration of psychotherapy approaches?

11. Summarize current issues in the field of community psychology.

ANSWERS TO SELF-TEST, CHAPTER 17

MULTIPLE CHOICE

1. d (p. 566)	2. c. (p. 568)	3. c (p. 568)	4. b (p. 568)
5. d (p. 569)	6. d (p. 573)	7. a (p. 578)	8. d (p. 578)
9. d (p. 591)	10. d (p. 593)	11. b (p. 595)	12. d (p. 593)

SHORT ANSWER

1. An international group of leading psychotherapy researchers was given a survey that asked each researcher to indicate their degree of agreement with 20 statements about psychotherapy, based on existing research. The experts demonstrated strong agreement that research supported the following claims:

   - Therapy is helpful to the majority of clients,
   - Most people achieve some change relatively quickly in therapy.
   - In general, therapies achieve similar outcomes (i.e., the Dodo bird effect).
   - People change more due to "common factors" than to "specific factors" associated with therapies.
   - The client-therapist relationship is the best predictor of treatment change.
   - Most therapists learn more about effective therapy techniques from their experience rather than from research.
   - About 10 percent of clients get worse as a result of therapy. (p. 568)

2. Ego analysts emphasize current, conscious ego functions that do not directly depend on id energies. Thus, they see people more as being able to control current environment and less as being pushed by unconscious drives. (p. 571)

3. Rogers says healthy people are aware of their own desires and fears. They recognize and pursue their own goals. That is, they march to the beat of their own drum. (p. 575)

4. The text concludes that it is useful for clinicians to develop such qualities but research does not prove that simply having them is sufficient to produce change. (p. 576)

5. A central component of MI is the use of CBT techniques to challenge the perceived benefits of the problem behaviour, within the context of an empathetic relationship with the therapist. The focus is on changing the value of negative behaviours and increasing the value of positive, adaptive behaviours through a dialogue with the client about these very issues. (p. 576)

6. Approach therapy using the methods, approaches, and results of experimental psychology. (p. 578)

7. The essence of EFT is that marital distress stems from maladaptive and distressed forms of emotion in the marital context and from the destructive interactions that result from this maladaptive emotion. (p. 587)

8. Conflicts are inevitable when people live together. They are best addressed by involving all the family and focusing on communication. (p. 588)

9.   Present problematic behaviour both reflects and maintains childhood conflicts. That is, childhood conflicts contribute to present behaviour and, in turn, the results of present behaviour reconfirm the childhood conflicts. (p. 591)

10.   We could lose important theoretical distinctions and thus treatment options. Distinctions may be issues that need to be studied and perhaps someday integrated, not just blurred over. (p. 592)

11.   The field seeks social change but it is not clear (a) how to do so and (b) how to decide what changes to seek, especially when social or ethical values are involved. (p. 593)

Chapter 18 Legal and Ethical Issues

OVERVIEW

The last section of the text consists of two chapters discussing issues in abnormal psychology. The previous chapter covered issues in psychological intervention. It reviewed approaches to intervention and attempts to integrate them. This, the final chapter of the text, turns to legal and ethical issues in abnormal psychology. In studying this chapter, remember that "issues" do not have easy solutions—or they wouldn't be issues. Especially in working with human beings, there are often no easy answers. Thus, it is important to anticipate when issues will occur and to understand the differences, implications, and options in order to handle them as effectively as possible.

CHAPTER SUMMARY

In Canada, there is a continual and sometimes subtle interplay between the legal and mental health systems that starts with the protection of the mentally disabled in the Canadian Charter of Rights and Freedoms. In this interplay, psychologists and other mental health workers struggle with many legal and ethical issues or dilemmas. Legal issues develop when an individual's mental condition becomes an issue in court. In *Criminal Commitment* cases, issues develop when individuals accused of crimes are found incompetent to stand trial or are acquitted by reason of insanity at the time of the crime. In *Civil Commitment* cases, individuals not accused of crimes may be committed to institutions if they are considered mentally ill and dangerous to themselves or others. Debate continues on whether these legal procedures are fair to the individuals involved and to larger society. Recent court rulings have clarified the legal rights of committed individuals, especially those civilly committed. These include rights to be treated in the least restrictive environment possible, to receive real treatment, and to refuse treatment in some cases. Debate continues on how to protect individual freedoms while protecting society from disturbed individuals.

Ethical Dilemmas in Therapy and Research covers the very broad area of individual rights. For example, psychologists recognize ethical obligations to obtain the informed consent before involving people in research and treatment. Yet research participants might behave differently if they completely understood what was being investigated. Further, disturbed patients, under pressure from family and society, may not be able to choose freely or even to understand the consequences of their decisions. Therapists are also ethically and legally obligated to respect the confidentiality of their patients, yet they may have to break confidentiality if, for example, patients are endangering themselves or others. Other dilemmas arise when therapy clients recover memories of childhood abuse. Such problems are true ethical dilemmas that do not always have easy answers.

ESSENTIAL CONCEPTS

1. Section 15 (1) of the Canadian Charter of Rights and Freedoms (i.e. equality before and under law) is especially significant because it extends the right of equality to mentally ill people.

2. Criminal commitment applies to individuals suspected of being mentally ill and of breaking laws, while civil commitment procedures apply to individuals suspected of being mentally ill and dangerous.

3. The insanity defence deals with an individual's mental state at the time of a crime. Criteria of insanity continue to evolve and to be controversial. The term currently used in Canadian law (section 16 of the Criminal Code) is "not criminally responsible."

4. Competency deals with an individual's mental state at the time of trial. It also raises difficult issues.

5. Laws governing civil commitment vary, but generally, a person can be committed if they are (a) mentally ill and (b) a danger to themselves or others. One controversial issue that has arisen in Canada involves the notion of "involuntary community commitment" and the concept of community treatment orders to ensure treatment compliance.

6. In the Starson ruling, the Supreme Court of Canada upheld a mental patient's right to refuse treatment even if involuntarily committed under a Canadian mental health act.

7. There is debate as to how accurately mental health professionals can predict the future dangerousness of a mentally disturbed individual.

8. Legal proceedings have addressed the rights of people committed through criminal and civil proceedings. These include the right to care in the least restrictive alternate setting, the right to treatment (not just minimal custodial care), and the right to refuse especially dangerous or noxious treatments.

9. Deinstitutionalization is an effort to get committed people out of mental hospitals. Unfortunately, it has led to other problems, including homelessness.

10. Psychologists also face difficult ethical dilemmas in dealing with research participants and patients.

11. Regulations have been formulated to protect the rights of subjects in psychological research, such as the concept of informed consent—informing the subject of the risks involved in the research and of their right to freely accept or reject participation in the experiment.

12. The ethical codes of various mental health professions dictate that, with certain exceptions, communications between patient and therapist must be confidential. Privileged communication laws extend this protection into the courts.

13. Therapists face additional ethical dilemmas in determining who is the client whose interests they should serve, what the goals for treatment should be, and what techniques may be justified to achieve those goals.

14. Recently, therapists have confronted additional dilemmas with clients who recover memories of abuse. Protecting rights of both the alleged victim and alleged perpetrator is complex.

KEY TERMS

civil commitment (p. 601)

insanity defence (p. 602)

confidentiality (p. 628)

M'Naghten Rules (p. 603)

community commitment (p. 609)

not criminally responsible (p. 602)

criminal commitment (p. 601)

prior capable wish (p. 619)

informed consent (p. 627)

privileged communication (p. 616)

STUDY QUESTIONS

CRIMINAL COMMITMENT (p. 601)

1. What unique status do the mentally ill have in Canada due to the Canadian Charter of Rights and Freedoms? (p. 621)

2. What legal assumption underlies the defence of "not criminally responsible due to a mental disorder"? Trace the history of this defence using five landmark cases, guidelines, and laws. Describe two recent changes (since 1990). Summarize three general points regarding insanity, mental illness, and the concept of "not criminally responsible." (p. 602)

3. Summarize the case of *Regina vs. Swain* (1991). Explain the changes in Canadian law that were derived from this decision and incorporated into Bill C-30 (1991). (p. 604)

4. Distinguish between "insanity" and "competency." What is the basic legal principle behind fitness to stand trial? (p. 604)

CIVIL COMMITMENT (p. 606)

5. Identify the principle underlying civil commitment, the common criteria, and the common types of commitment procedures. Describe the general outlines of "involuntary admission" under the Canadian mental health acts. To what degree do provisions differ from province to province? List the criteria for community treatment orders to be issued in Saskatchewan. (p. 608)

6. How dangerous are former mental patients? Evaluate traditional research on and practical criteria for predicting dangerousness. Describe more recent research on predicting dangerousness and ways to control potentially dangerous former patients. (p. 612)

7. Why are courts protecting rights of individuals threatened with involuntary commitment? (p. 618)

8. Summarize three recent trends protecting the rights of individuals who have been committed. How do ethical free will issues underlie these trends? Summarize the impact of *Regina v. Rogers* (1991). How do Paul and Lentz propose to deal with these seemingly contradictory rights? (p. 619)

9. What factors led to deinstitutionalization policies? What were the unintended results? What future do Gralnick and others fear? (p. 621)

ETHICAL DILEMMAS IN THERAPY AND RESEARCH (p. 625)

10. Give three examples outside psychology that point to the need for ethical restraints in research. In current research, what process protects participants, and what two recent developments threaten that protection? (p. 625)

11. Summarize five ethical dilemmas and point out why each is a dilemma (i.e., why it is not easily resolved). (p. 625) Distinguish between confidentiality and privileged communication. (p. 628)

12. Summarize the ethical and legal issues involved in reports of recovered memories. Summarize the textbook's concluding comments. (p. 631)

SELF-TEST, CHAPTER 18

(* Items not covered in Study Questions.)

MULTIPLE CHOICE

1. The Canadian Charter of Rights and Freedoms is almost unique in the world because of
    a. the protection it extents to the mentally ill.
    b. the lack of protection it affords the mentally ill.
    c. the protection it extends to the criminally impaired.
    d. the lack of protection it affords the elderly.

2. Criminal and civil commitment can be best distinguished by
    a. whether the one being committed is insane.
    b. whether a crime has been committed by the individual.
    c. the severity of the symptoms and the crime committed.
    d. the type of police intervention necessary.

3. One of the changes brought about by *Regina v. Swain* was
    a. provision for holding individuals found not criminally responsible in mental hospitals.
    b. mandatory notification of communities when mentally ill individuals were released from prison.

   c.   provisions for allowing registered psychologists to testify in trials involving the insanity defense.

   d.   provisions in law for distinguishing mental state at the time of the crime vs. the time of the trial.

4.   In *Winko v. British Columbia*, the B.C. Supreme Court decided that

   a.   if it cannot be determined whether a mentally disordered person is a threat to public safety, he or she must be discharged.

   b.   only a psychiatrist can make a determination with regard to the dangerousness of an individual.

   c.   only if he or she had previously committed a violent crime can an individual be held involuntarily in a mental institution.

   d.   only objective measures of dangerousness may be introduced into a court proceeding.

5.   When someone is determined incompetent to stand trial, what typically happens to them?

   a.   They are released.

   b.   They are treated, then tried for the original crime.

   c.   They are treated, then released.

   d.   They are treated while serving time in prison for the crime.

6.   Which of the following is not a criterion used in Saskatchewan for community treatment orders (CTO)?

   a.   The person must have a mental disorder.

   b.   The person may harm themselves or others.

   c.   The person is incapable of complying with requirements of the CTO.

   d.   The person is incapable of making an informed decision.

7.   Monahan suggests that the prediction of violence is most accurate under which of the following conditions?

   a.   non-emergency situations

   b.   when the person is currently in the hospital because of past dangerous behaviour

   c.   in an emergency, when violence appears imminent

   d.   when a person can be evaluated over a period of time by several professionals in a controlled environment

*8.   The Tarasoff decision has created concerns over duty to warn in which of the following situations?

   a.   Sam, who has indicated to his therapist that he may abuse his children when angry

   b.   Tony, who is HIV-positive, and continues to engage in unprotected sex

   c.   Alison, who has threatened to destroy her ex-boyfriend's car

   d.   All of the above are recent issues that have been considered under the Tarasoff decision.

9.   In *Regina v. Rogers* (1991), B.C. courts reiterated the rights of

   a.   criminals to a jury trial even when using the insanity defense.

   b.   mentally disordered individuals to refuse treatment even if admitted involuntarily.

   c.   hospitals to refuse to treat dangerous patients.

   d.   hospitals to refuse to house convicted ciminals.

10. In the Starson decision, the Supreme Court of Canada ruled that individuals involuntarily admitted to a mental health facility under a Canadian mental health act

    a. lose the right to refuse treatment.

    b. retain the right to refuse treatment for physical disorders but not mental disorders.

    c. retain the right to refuse treatment.

    d. must have a court-appointed guardian who can make decisions regarding mental treatments.

11. Deinstitutionalization has been described as an improper label because

    a. most patients end up in treatment in outpatient clinics, thus visiting other institutions.

    b. most deinstitutionalized patients remain mentally ill.

    c. patients typically end up in other long-term care institutions.

    d. few patients are actually discharged from the hospital.

12. Human subjects committees and institutional review boards

    a. have been proposed by the American Psychological Association.

    b. have been outlawed since the Nuremburg war trials.

    c. are used to ensure that subjects participate in scientifically significant research.

    d. are used to protect the safety and rights of research subjects.

13. Confidentiality is based on _____, whereas a privileged communication is _____.

    a. provincial law; decided by the individual therapist.

    b. the ethical code of a profession; based on law.

    c. the therapist's obligation not to disclose information; the client's obligation not to disclose opinions about the therapist.

    d. verbal report in therapy; a written report of the therapist's impression of a client.

14. Which of the following was the most significant ethical error made by the Montreux Clinic?

    a. sexual abuse of residents by staff

    b. financial abuse of residents

    c. use of over-qualified staff

    d. forcing treatment on residents

SHORT ANSWER

1. Summarize the issue in the M'Naghten ruling defining criminal insanity.

2. Summarize the case of *Regina v. Swain*.

3. Describe the criteria for the Fitness Interview Test Revised.

4. On what basis may individuals be committed to a mental hospital against their will (civil commitment)?

5.   How dangerous are former mental patients?

6.   Describe Rice's conclusion regarding the efficacy of treatment programs for psychopaths.

7.   What is the ethical issue in "informed consent"?

8.   Give several reasons (the text lists four) why therapists may reveal things clients tell them even when state law provides privileged communication for therapy relationships.

9.   Describe the ethical issue of "who is the client."

10.   What is the ethical issue in reports of recovered memories of child abuse?

ANSWERS TO SELF-TEST, CHAPTER 18

MULTIPLE CHOICE

1. a (p. 601)	2. b (p. 601)	3. d (p. 603)	4. a (p. 603)
5. b (p. 604)	6. c (p. 609)	7. c (p. 612)	8. d (p. 616)
9. b (p. 619)	10. c (p. 619)	11. c (p. 620)	12. d (p. 626)
13. b (p. 628)	14. d (p. 630)		

SHORT ANSWER

1.   The basic issue in the 1843 M'Naghten ruling was the ability of M'Naghten to understand the nature and quality of the act he was doing. The court ruled that he couldn't because of the disease of the mind he was suffering at the time of the crime. (p. 603)

2.   Swain threatened his family and was arrested for assault causing bodily harm. He testified that he was trying to save his family from the devil and was found not guilty by reason of insanity. At the time, there was no provision in the law distinguishing between an individual's mental state at the time of the crime versus at the time of the trial. In addition, even though he had recovered from his illness, Swain's detention contravened Section 9 of the Charter of Rights and Freedoms. The Supreme Court of Canada ordered the government to enact legislation correcting these omissions. (p. 603)

3.   The FIT-R assess the person's understanding of the nature and purpose of the legal proceedings, the likely consequences of the proceedings, and the person's ability to communicate with his or her lawyer. (p. 606)

4.   Civil commitment occurs if they are mentally ill and dangerous to others or themselves (which may include being unable to take care of themselves). (p. 606)

5.   Despite stereotypes, research indicates they are usually no more dangerous than people in general. The exception is substance abusers, who are more likely to be dangerous (whether ex-patients or not). (p. 612)

6.   Rice is quite pessimistic about the chances of treating and rehabilitating psychopaths due in part to her findings that treatment actually raises their recidivism rates. (p. 614)

7.   People may feel pressured into consenting or may not understand what they're consenting to. Thus their "consent" may be meaningless. (p. 626)

8.   (a) Client files suit against therapist, (b) client is being abused, (c) client started therapy to evade law, (d) client is dangerous to self or others. (p. 628)

9.   This refers to situations where the therapist has responsibility to several individuals or entities whose interests may differ. A therapist may not be able to serve both sets of interests. (p. 628)

10.   There are dangers both in encouraging and discouraging clients to recover memories. Encouragement could lead to false diagnosis. Discouragement could mean the memory remains repressed but hampers the client's current life. (p. 631)